SMOKING

Other Books in the At Issue Series:

DISCARDED

SMOKING

Mary E. Williams, *Book Editor*

David L. Bender, *Publisher*
Bruno Leone, *Executive Editor*

Bonnie Szumski, *Editorial Director*
David M. Haugen, *Managing Editor*

An Opposing Viewpoints® Series

Greenhaven Press, Inc.
San Diego, California

Library of Congress Cataloging-in-Publication Data

Smoking / Mary E. Williams, book editor.
        p.   cm. — (At issue)
    Includes bibliographical references and index.
    ISBN 0-7377-0156-0 (pbk. bdg. : alk. paper). —
ISBN 0-7377-0157-9 (lib. : alk. paper)
    1. Tobacco habit—United States. 2. Cigarette habit—United States. 3. Smoking—United States. 4. Tobacco industry—United States. I. Williams, Mary E., 1960–   . II. Series: At issue (San Diego, Calif.)
HV5760.S665   2000
362.29'6—dc21   99-33070
                                                                                      CIP

©2000 by Greenhaven Press, Inc., PO Box 289009,
San Diego, CA 92198-9009

Printed in the U.S.A.

Every effort has been made to trace owners of copyrighted material.

Table of Contents

Introduction

On November 23, 1998, the nation's four largest tobacco companies agreed to pay forty-six states a total of $206 billion and adhere to advertising and marketing restrictions in a negotiated deal that turned out to be the largest civil lawsuit settlement in history. This settlement was a result of dozens of suits filed against the tobacco industry in the 1990s by state attorneys general attempting to recover the health care costs of treating smoking-related illnesses. In many ways, this 1998 settlement was also the outcome of a decades-long effort on the part of public health advocates, antismoking activists, and legislators to regulate tobacco and reduce smoking. Since the U.S. Surgeon General first declared smoking a health risk in 1964, many physicians and public health experts have been involved in a broad campaign against cigarette consumption. The tobacco industry, however, along with many smokers and others who believe that antitobacco activism misdirects national priorities, have actively opposed this antismoking drive.

Many private and governmental factions have condemned smoking as a health risk since the 1964 Surgeon General's report on smoking and health linked smoking to cancer. Medical experts, antismoking activists, and lawmakers have worked to pass a variety of regulations designed to reduce smoking. Some efforts have focused on the labeling of cigarette packages and on cigarette advertising. The first labeling law, the Cigarette Labeling and Advertising Act, took effect in 1966. It required cigarette packages and advertisements to warn that cigarette smoking "may be hazardous to your health." Another early legislative restriction was the 1969 Public Health Cigarette Smoking Act, which banned cigarette advertising on television and radio, leaving the tobacco industry only the print media and billboards on which to advertise. In 1970, the Supreme Court upheld this ban in the face of a challenge by the tobacco industry. The cigarette package warning label was also strengthened to read, "Warning: The Surgeon General has determined that cigarette smoking is dangerous to your health." In 1984, the Comprehensive Smoking Education Act required the use of several different warning labels, which are rotated sequentially.

Government agencies also began to ban smoking in public spaces. In 1973, the Civil Aeronautics Board began requiring commercial airlines to offer nonsmoking sections. Later, smoking was banned on domestic flights of under two hours; and, in 1990, it was banned on all domestic flights of six hours or less. Also in 1973, Arizona became the first state to prohibit smoking in some public places. Several other states followed suit; and, in 1987, the Department of Health and Human Services, a federal agency, started banning smoking in its offices. In 1993, the Environmental Protection Agency (EPA) released a report that linked environmental, or secondhand, tobacco smoke with cancer and other diseases among nonsmokers. The EPA report provided the necessary grounds for some legislators to propose a ban on smoking in most nonresidential buildings. As a result, in 1998, California became the first state in the nation to ban cigarette smoking in bars, private clubs, and card clubs. Smoking had been prohibited in California restaurants and indoor workplaces since 1995; with the 1998 law, nearly all indoor spaces in the state are smoke-free.

These antismoking successes helped to set the stage for the most recent antitobacco efforts. Moreover, several studies conducted in the last three decades of the twentieth century confirm that long-term cigarette smoking causes emphysema, lung cancer, and heart disease. The Centers for Disease Control and Prevention, for example, estimates that more than 400,000 Americans die each year from smoking-related illnesses. Furthermore, reports the American Lung Association, the U.S. economy has lost nearly $100 billion in health care costs and diminished productivity due to smoking. States have traditionally paid for a part of these costs through Medicaid, a governmental health insurance program for the needy. However, in May 1994, the state of Mississippi decided to sue the tobacco industry to recover Medicaid costs for treating diseases caused by smoking. Soon afterward, more than forty states followed Mississippi's example.

At first, cigarette companies declared that they would fight these lawsuits in court. In the past, the tobacco industry had won lawsuits filed by those who claimed that cigarette manufacturers were liable for their smoking-related illnesses. Tobacco industry lawyers had successfully argued that citizens were well aware of the health risks associated with regular smoking and that the required Surgeon General's warning on cigarette packages consistently reminded smokers of the dangers of their habit. Those who chose to smoke in spite of these warnings, maintained the tobacco industry, were solely responsible for their decision to consume a health-damaging product.

In the late 1990s, however, several discoveries weakened the tobacco industry's argument and increased cigarette companies' willingness to negotiate settlements with litigants. For one thing, newly released tobacco company documents proved that cigarette manufacturers had for decades intentionally suppressed evidence about the hazards of smoking. Furthermore, former tobacco company workers stepped forward to testify that their employers had downplayed their awareness of the addictive nature of nicotine—yet had also experimented with manipulating nicotine levels in cigarettes to "hook" more smokers. In addition, previously secret industry documents revealed that tobacco companies intentionally—and illegally—targeted minors in their marketing campaigns. One R.J. Reynolds memorandum from 1975, for example, proclaims that "[Camel filters] must increase its share penetration among the 14–24 age group, which have a new set of more liberal values and which represent tomorrow's cigarette business."

These findings led to allegations that tobacco companies had perpetrated fraud by concealing important information about the nature of their products and marketing techniques. The states suing the tobacco industry asserted that since cigarette manufacturers had intentionally suppressed data that might have discouraged people from smoking, the cigarette industry was at least partly blamable for causing smoking-related illnesses.

In June 1997, the tobacco industry negotiated a preliminary agreement with forty of the states that had filed lawsuits. As part of the proposed settlement, the major cigarette manufacturers agreed to limit their marketing activities, initiate a campaign to reduce underage smoking, and submit to potential Food and Drug Administration (FDA) regulation of tobacco. In return, the tobacco industry would be granted immunity from future class action suits, and a limit would be placed on any damages won from individual lawsuits.

Some public health advocates welcomed the proposed settlement, claiming that it would lower teen smoking rates and effectively punish the tobacco industry for deceiving the public about the dangers of smoking. Others, however, sharply criticized the settlement for being too lenient on the tobacco industry. They argued that the agreement would actually cater to the tobacco companies' financial interests by protecting them from expensive liability lawsuits. Since the 1997 settlement was subject to congressional approval, lawmakers who were critical of the preliminary agreement drafted legislation that would expand the scope of the original plan. Republican senator John McCain's antismoking bill, entitled the National Tobacco Policy and Youth Smoking Reduction Act, demanded the tobacco companies to pay $516 billion over a twenty-five year period into a government fund—money that would reimburse states for smoking-related health care costs and pay for antismoking programs and research. McCain's bill also requested a significant tax increase on cigarettes, the banning of outdoor advertising and ads using cartoon, animal, or human figures, an end to cigarette vending machines, and a requirement that the tobacco industry reduce the youth smoking rate by 60 percent over ten years. Moreover, the bill reduced the tobacco industry's liability protections that had been proposed in the 1997 agreement.

McCain's bill was strongly opposed by the tobacco industry. In the spring of 1998, the four major tobacco companies—Philip Morris, R.J. Reynolds, British and American Tobacco (owners of Brown and Williamson), and Loews—withdrew from negotiations. The McCain bill was unacceptable, they argued, because it did not provide enough liability protections and would eventually drive the tobacco industry out of business. The tobacco companies then placed full-page ads in the nation's major newspapers, contending that McCain's bill would place unconstitutional restrictions on tobacco advertising, launch new government bureaucracies to regulate products containing nicotine, create "half a trillion dollars in new taxes," and "devastate the tobacco industry." In the meantime, legislators became increasingly divided over the tobacco bill. Republicans and Democrats disagreed on how to allocate the $516 billion that would be raised as a result of the legislation. Also of concern was the amount of assistance that would be offered to tobacco farmers who would inevitably be affected by the passage of the bill. In the end, McCain's tobacco legislation was rejected by the Senate in June 1998.

Although federal tobacco control legislation failed, the settlement eventually reached in November 1998 is loosely modeled on the June 1997 proposal. In addition to paying $206 billion to forty-six states over a twenty-five-year period, the tobacco industry has pledged to fund a $1.5 billion, five-year antismoking campaign that includes research and public education programs. In addition, cigarette manufacturers have agreed to certain marketing restrictions, including an end to the use of cartoon characters in ads, large-scale outdoor advertising, and the sale of logo-emblazoned merchandise. Moreover, tobacco labels can no longer sponsor most concerts, youth teams, and sporting events. The tobacco industry now has protection against any future state lawsuits, although individual smokers can still sue.

Public health advocates have mixed feelings about the tobacco settlement. Cass Wheeler of the American Heart Association captured the public health community's sentiments regarding the tobacco settlement with these words: "Perfect? No. A beginning? Yes." Most antitobacco activists are pleased that the states will receive compensation for the medical costs of treating illnesses caused by cigarette smoking. But some feel that the settlement was a kind of victory for tobacco companies, as they will be shielded from many potentially damaging liability lawsuits. Others are concerned about loopholes in the settlement which still allow significant amounts of advertising to reach teenagers. For example, each tobacco company can still sponsor one brand-name event each year, such as Brown and Williamson's Kool Jazz Festival. Cigarette companies can also promote their products within these annual events—including posters lauding the company's support and brand names painted on race cars. Moreover, outdoor advertising that emphasizes tobacco-company sponsorship is allowed ninety days before an annual event. Hubert H. Humphrey III, attorney general of Minnesota, contends that the settlement "demonstrates how far we have to go." He maintains that legislators must create provisions "that would keep track of tobacco use by minors and penalize the industry if it does not decline." Moreover, Humphrey argues, since the tobacco industry is likely to "fight to keep their customers addicted . . . Congress must grant regulatory authority over nicotine to the [FDA]."

Some critics of the tobacco settlement are appalled at the amount of time, energy, and expense that has been invested in battling an industry that manufactures a legal product. Many of these critics contend that the health dangers of smoking have actually been exaggerated in order to advance the antitobacco agenda. Retired scientist Rosalind B. Marimont maintains that "by vastly overrating the dangers of tobacco . . . [antismoking groups] have gravely distorted the proper priorities for our resources." Los Angeles radio talk-show host Dennis Prager also argues that the "war on tobacco" represents a dangerous misplacement of moral values: "The next generation will ask: What preoccupied America in the final decade of the twentieth century—while unprecedented numbers of its children were being raised without fathers, while the country was living with rates of murder far higher than in any other advanced democracy . . . [while] rogue nations built stockpiles of chemical and biological weapons . . . ? The majority of [America's] national politicians, state attorneys general and educators will be able to answer together, 'We fought tobacco.' Shame on them all."

In the years to come, the battle between the public health community and the tobacco industry will continue as antismoking advocates continue to push for federally mandated controls on nicotine and tobacco products. Antitobacco activists hope to use the 1998 tobacco settlement as leverage for future tobacco control legislation, and in March

1999, Bill Clinton's administration began assembling a task force to prepare a lawsuit against the tobacco industry to recover federal costs related to the care of those with smoking-related illnesses. *At Issue: Smoking* provides an overview of this continuing controversy as authors debate the health effects of smoking as well as the responses of scientists, industry supporters, consumer advocates, and lawmakers to the marketing and consumption of cigarettes.

1

The Surgeons General and Smoking: An Overview

John Parascandola

John Parascandola is the director of the Office of Public Health History in the Department of Health and Human Services, a branch of the United States Public Health Service.

In the 1930s, the increased incidence of lung cancer compelled scientists and physicians to examine more closely the speculation that smoking caused cancer. Critics countered that other factors, such as pollution, could be responsible for the rise in lung cancer; however, in the 1950s, medical researchers from the United States and Britain defined smoking as a major cause of the rising rates of lung cancer. In the early 1960s, antitobacco activists and public health organizations urged the U.S. government to create an advisory group of experts to study the health effects of smoking. This group, known as the Surgeon General's Advisory Committee on Smoking and Health, identified cigarette smoking as a significant health hazard. The Advisory Committee's conclusions sparked a strong antismoking campaign that resulted in an overall decrease in cigarette consumption.

O n January 11, 1964, a most unusual press conference was held behind closed doors in the State Department auditorium to release the report of the Surgeon General's Committee on Smoking and Health. The press conference was held on a Saturday to minimize the effects of the report on the stock market and to ensure coverage in the Sunday newspapers. All of the approximately 200 reporters attending were required to remain for the entire session. Each was given a copy of the final report and allowed to study it for about an hour. Reporters were then permitted to question the Surgeon General and the committee members about the report. Finally the doors were opened and the reporters raced out to file their stories. Surgeon General Luther Terry later recalled: "The report hit the country like a bombshell. It was front page news and the lead story on every radio and television station in the United States and many abroad."

Reprinted from John Parascandola, "The Surgeons General and Smoking," *Public Health Reports*, September 19, 1997, published by the U.S. Department of Health and Human Services.

Antismoking history

That report is now viewed, and justly so, as a milestone in the campaign against tobacco in this country. However, this famous 1964 report was not the first time that the name of a Public Health Service Surgeon General was associated with a statement about the health hazards of tobacco. As quoted by Republican Senator Reed Smoot of Utah in a June 10, 1929, speech on the Senate floor, Surgeon General Hugh Cumming claimed that cigarettes tended to cause nervousness, insomnia, and other ill effects in women. He warned that smoking could lower the "physical tone" of the nation. Smoot was calling upon the authority of the Surgeon General in an unsuccessful attempt to push the Senate to pass a bill that he had introduced to bring tobacco under the regulations of the Food and Drug Administration.

Admittedly, Surgeon General Cumming's condemnation of smoking was rather a weak one. It was, first of all, aimed only at women smokers. Like many other physicians of his time, Cumming believed that women were more susceptible than men to certain injuries, especially of the nervous system. While he was not convinced that smoking by women was harmful in all cases, he was concerned about the damage that excessive smoking might do to young women. Cumming, a smoker himself, also wished to distance himself from the more vociferous of the anti-tobacco reformers of the day, many of whom were also associated with the temperance movement. What apparently motivated him to speak out was aggressive advertising aimed at women and young people.

Although [there] were careful studies involving hundreds of patients, the research did not convince everyone that there was indeed a causal connection between smoking and lung cancer.

Cumming's rather limited attack on cigarettes does not appear to have had any significant consequences. It is merely an interesting footnote in the history of the campaign against smoking. His view was typical of physicians of the 1920s: smoking was not seen as a significant health threat for most people. However, the evidence that was eventually to convince the American medical profession and the general public that smoking was indeed hazardous to one's health slowly began to accumulate.

It had long been suspected by some that cigarettes might be carcinogenic, but it was only in the 1930s, when physicians began to encounter cases of lung cancer with increased frequency, that the issue received more significant attention. As early as 1932, Dr. William McNally of Rush Medical College suggested that cigarette smoking was an important factor in the higher rates of lung cancer. In 1938, in an article in the *Science News Letter*, Drs. Alton Ochsner and Michael DeBakey of New Orleans wrote: "More persons are dying of cancer of the lungs than ever before, probably because more persons are smoking and inhaling tobacco smoke than ever before." Ochsner continued to make this case throughout the

1940s, but he was dismissed by many of his colleagues as an antismoking enthusiast since he forbade his own staff from smoking.

Skepticism about linking cancer to smoking

Not everyone accepted the premise that the rise in the incidence of lung cancer was linked to cigarette smoking. Many physicians and scientists were skeptical about the epidemiological evidence. A statistical correlation between an increase in cigarette smoking and an increase in lung cancer does not prove that there is a causal connection. A prominent physician, Evarts Graham, who had been one of Ochsner's teachers, noted, "Yes, there is a parallel between the sale of cigarettes and the incidence of cancer of the lung, but there is also a parallel between the sale of nylon stockings and cancer of the lung." Graham eventually did become more convinced of the connection between smoking and lung cancer.

Critics of the view that lung cancer was linked to smoking argued that other factors, such as increasing atmospheric pollution from automobile exhausts, might also explain the rise in the incidence of the disease. Some physicians even argued that the incidence of lung cancer only appeared to be increasing because better diagnostic tools were making it easier to identify.

In 1950, Wynder and the above mentioned Graham (in this country) and Doll and Hill (in England) published preliminary reports of independent studies showing an association between smoking cigarettes and lung cancer. The Americans would only cautiously state that extensive and prolonged smoking, especially of cigarettes, seemed to be an important factor in the inducement of lung cancer. The British researchers asserted somewhat definitely that smoking was an important factor in the production of lung cancer. They admitted, however, that other factors could also cause the disease.

Although these were careful studies involving hundreds of patients, the research did not convince everyone that there was indeed a causal connection between smoking and lung cancer. The studies were criticized, for example, because they were retrospective and hence relied heavily on the recollections of patients. Even Graham himself did not quit smoking, although he cut back to a pack a day in 1953. Unfortunately, he died of lung cancer four years later.

Evidence for the case against smoking

But other research, both epidemiological and pathological, soon provided further evidence for the case against smoking. One particularly significant study by Hammond and Horn, funded by the American Cancer Society, was based on a prospective design that involved use of volunteers to locate hundreds of thousands of smokers and nonsmokers and to track their health over time. Even the early results, published beginning in 1954, showed that age-adjusted death rates were at least three times higher among male smokers than among nonsmokers and five times higher for heavy smokers. Interestingly, both authors were themselves smokers and gave up cigarettes in favor of pipe smoking as a result of their research.

This research eventually began to be reflected in public policy statements. In June 1957, after reviewing the report of a Study Group in which Public Health Service (PHS) had participated, Surgeon General Leroy Burney issued a statement about the health effects of smoking. Although noting that more research on the subject was needed, Burney concluded:

> While there are naturally differences of opinion in interpreting the data on lung cancer and cigarette smoking, the Public Health Service feels the weight of the evidence is increasingly pointing in one direction: that excessive smoking is one of the causative factors in lung cancer.

That same year, the Medical Research Council in Britain reported that a major part of the increase in lung cancer in that country and other nations could be attributed to smoking. In 1959, Surgeon General Burney expanded on his 1957 statement in an article about smoking and lung cancer. Speaking on behalf of PHS, Burney clearly stated that the weight of evidence implicated smoking as "the principal etiological factor in the increased incidence of lung cancer." Smoking had thus gone from being one of the causative factors to being the principal causative factor in the increased incidence of lung cancer.

The [Surgeon General's Advisory] Committee concluded that "cigarette smoking is a health hazard of sufficient importance to the United States to warrant appropriate remedial action."

As the nation entered the 1960s, anti-tobacco activists pressed for more effective action to curb smoking. On June 1, 1961, the presidents of the American Cancer Society, the American Public Health Association, the American Heart Association, and the National Tuberculosis Association wrote to President John Kennedy urging him to establish a commission to study the health effects of smoking. The President referred the letter to the Department of Health, Education, and Welfare, and in January 1962 representatives of the four organizations met with Surgeon General Luther Terry. This meeting eventually led to a decision to form an advisory committee of experts to study the matter of smoking and health.

In July 1962, Terry met with representatives of various health organizations and the Tobacco Institute (representing the tobacco companies) to define the work of the advisory group and to suggest people to serve on it. A list of more than 150 names was compiled. Terry shrewdly recognized that the group would need broad support so each of the organizations involved in the meeting (including the Tobacco Institute) had an opportunity to veto any of the names. In addition, anyone who had taken a public position on the issue of smoking and health was eliminated from consideration.

Terry selected 10 people to serve as the Surgeon General's Advisory Committee on Smoking and Health. Eight of the members held MD degrees, with three of that group holding PhD degrees as well. The other two members were a PhD chemist and a statistician. Three of the members smoked cigarettes, and two others smoked pipes or cigars. Terry, himself a smoker, served as the nominal Chairman of the group, but it was agreed that he would not participate in any of its deliberations or conclusions.

The Advisory Committee worked for a little over a year, meeting periodically, reviewing all of the available data, and receiving input from a large number of consultants and organizations. The Committee was also assigned a small staff to assist with the work. Finally, on January 11, 1964, the Committee released its report. Since a decision had been made not to have a minority report, only conclusions that all Committee members could accept were included.

The report implicated smoking in a number of disease conditions. Among the main conclusions were that cigarette smoking was causally related to lung cancer in men (and probably in women as well), that it was a significant factor in the causation of laryngeal cancer, and that it was the most important cause of chronic bronchitis.

In some cases, such as coronary artery disease, the Committee noted that the evidence showed an association between smoking and a particular health problem but that a causal relationship had not been proved. The Committee's report also concluded that smoking was a habit rather than an addiction. Overall, the Committee concluded that "cigarette smoking is a health hazard of sufficient importance to the United States to warrant appropriate remedial action."

The Committee's report received widespread media coverage. *Newsweek* called the report "monumental," and the American Cancer Society stated that it was "a landmark in the history of man's fight against disease. The report also frightened many Americans into quitting or cutting down on smoking. Within three months of the issuance of the report, cigarette consumption had dropped about 20%, although it soon climbed back up to approximately its former level. It is fair to say, however, that the report initiated an intensive antismoking campaign that eventually led to a reduction in cigarette consumption. The most important function served by the report may have been as a rallying cry for the antismoking forces.

The [Surgeon General's] report initiated an intensive antismoking campaign that eventually led to a reduction in cigarette consumption.

A week after the release of the report, the Federal Trade Commission (FTC) proposed that a health warning be placed on cigarette packages and in advertisements. Before the proposed rules could go into effect, Congress passed the Cigarette Labeling and Advertising Act of 1965. Convinced that it would fare better in Congress than with the FTC, the tobacco industry had encouraged legislative action. The 1965 Act required a health warning on cigarette packages but suspended the FTC's proposed warnings in advertisements for four years (later extended to six). It also prohibited other Federal agencies from requiring health warnings in advertising and prohibited state and local governments from enacting requirements for more stringent regulations. The Act was thus a mixed blessing for the antismoking forces.

The Act also required the Secretary of Health, Education, and Welfare to submit annual reports to Congress on the health consequences of smoking, initiating the series of Surgeon General's reports for which the Office on Smoking and Health of the Centers for Disease Control and Prevention is presently responsible. In addition, the Act authorized the creation of a National Clearinghouse on Smoking and Health, the predecessor of the Office on Smoking and Health.

The position of Surgeon General has continued to be associated with the campaign against smoking, as was made especially visible during the tenure of C. Everett Koop, who was a forceful spokesperson about the health hazards of tobacco. It was the 1964 report, however, that firmly linked the name of the Surgeon General to the smoking issue.

2

Smoking Is Harmful

William F. Harrison

William F. Harrison is an obstetrician and gynecologist who practices at the Fayetteville Women's Clinic in Fayetteville, Arkansas.

Habitual cigarette smoking leads to serious health complications, including emphysema, cardiovascular disease, and various life-threatening cancers. Much of this damage occurs because tobacco smoke slowly destroys the cleansing mechanism in the lungs, allowing toxins to remain in prolonged contact with lung tissue. Moreover, the damage caused by exposure to tobacco smoke progresses more rapidly after many years of smoking, eventually resulting in the illnesses that cause more than 400,000 annual deaths in the United States alone.

M ost of us in medicine now accept that tobacco is associated with major health consequences and constitutes the No. 1 health problem in this country.

The consequences of smoking

What smokers have not yet come to terms with is that if they continue smoking, the probability of developing one or more of the major complications of smoking is 100%. It absolutely will happen. They will develop chronic bronchitis, laryngitis, pharyngitis, sinusitis and some degree of emphysema. It is also highly probable that they will develop serious disease in the arteries of all vital organs, including the brain and heart, markedly increasing their risk of heart attack and stroke. If they continue, they increase the probability of developing cancer of the lips, gums, tongue, pharynx, larynx, trachea, bronchi and lungs, of the bladder, cervix, gallbladder and other organs. Smoking contributes to rapid aging of the skin and connective tissues—women and men who smoke usually have the skin age of a person 10 to 20 years older than one who doesn't smoke, given the same degree of exposure to the sun.

About 415,000 people die prematurely each year in the U.S. as a result of smoking—the equivalent of 18 747s crashing every week with no survivors. Many of these victims die after long and excruciating illnesses,

Reprinted from William F. Harrison, "Why Stop Smoking? Let's Get Clinical," *Los Angeles Times*, editorials, July 7, 1996, by permission.

burdens to themselves, their families and society. The cost of this misery is incalculable, but we do know that the tobacco industry grosses about $50 billion a year from the agonies it inflicts.

How damage occurs

How does all this damage come about?

In normal lungs, the trachea and bronchi—the large and small tubes leading to the alveoli (the tiny sacs that do the actual work of the lungs)— are lined with a film of tissue that is one cell layer thick. The surface of these cells is covered with tiny, finger-like structures called cilia. These cilia beat constantly in a waving motion, which moves small particles and toxic substances out of the lung and into the back of the throat where they are swallowed. In a smoker or someone like a coal miner, who constantly breathes in large amounts of toxic substances, many of the cilia soon disappear. If exposure continues, some ciliated cells die and are replaced by squamous cells, the same type that form the skin. Without the cleansing function of the ciliated cells, toxic materials and particles are breathed further into the lungs, staying longer in contact with all the tissue. Each group of ciliated cells killed and replaced by squamous cells decreases by a certain fraction the lungs' ability to cleanse themselves. As this occurs, the amount of damage done by each cigarette increases to a greater and greater degree. By the time one has been a pack-a-day smoker for 10 years or so, extensive damage has already been done. By 20 years, much of the damage is irreversible and progresses more rapidly. After 10 years of smoking, each cigarette may do as much damage to the body as three or more packs did when a smoker first started.

After 10 years of smoking, each cigarette may do as much damage to the body as three or more packs did when a smoker first started.

The longer one smokes, the harder it gets to quit. Smoking is one of the most addictive of human habits, perhaps as addicting as crack cocaine or heroin. One has to quit every day, and there are no magic pills or crutches that make stopping easy. It is tough to do. Only those who keep trying ever quit. And even those who have smoked for only a short time or few cigarettes a day will probably find it difficult to stop. But the sooner a smoker makes this self-commitment, the more probable it is that he or she will quit before having done major damage to the body.

3

The Harmful Effects of Smoking Are Overstated

Rosalind B. Marimont

Rosalind B. Marimont is a retired mathematician and scientist living in Silver Spring, Maryland. She has been active in health policy issues for more than thirty years.

The health risks attributed to smoking have been grossly exaggerated. The Centers for Disease Control and Prevention (CDC) uses an erroneous computer application to estimate the number of deaths caused by smoking, leading the public to believe that 400,000 Americans die annually from smoking-related illnesses. In actuality, many of these deaths could be the result of other health problems, such as high cholesterol or obesity. The CDC's distorted information on the hazards of tobacco use, coupled with the strong antismoking sentiment in the U.S. government, has misdirected the nation's health priorities. The United States faces more dangers from violence, family breakdown, and drug abuse than it does from smoking.

In the War on Smoking, truth has been the first casualty. Junk science has replaced honest science, and propaganda parades as fact. By vastly overrating the dangers of tobacco, and neglecting those of alcohol and drugs, the Anti-Smoking Police (ASPs) have gravely distorted the proper priorities for our resources.

Faulty information about smoking

The "facts" now quoted as gospel by the ASPs are false. For example:
• *It is false that smoking kills 400,000 Americans annually*. This Centers for Disease Control (CDC) number is nothing but a computer-generated estimate by a program called SAMMEC [Smoking-Attributable Mortality, Morbidity, and Economic Cost], based on an erroneous model, ignoring all the rules of epidemiology, and vastly inflating the effects of smoking. For example, if Joe Smith is obese, has high cholesterol, diabetes, a fam-

Reprinted from Rosalind B. Marimont, "Casualties of the War on Smoking," web article on the FORCES website: www.forces.org/articles/files/roz-03.htm, by permission of the author.

ily history of heart attacks, never exercises, smokes, and dies of a heart attack, the CDC attributes his death to smoking only! SAMMEC is also the
basis for other scare numbers, such as that 3 million or 5 million of today's children will die from smoking.

• *It is false that smoking is a major danger to children. Children do not die
of tobacco related diseases.* If they smoke heavily they may die of lung cancer in their old age, 50 years from now, if lung cancer is still a threat. But
now and this year they are dying by the thousands in accidents, suicides,
and homicides, largely associated with drugs and alcohol. It is uncon-
scionable to keep diverting resources to the far future tobacco threat and
ignore the immediate drug and alcohol threat, which can kill them long
before they can get cancer!

• *It is false that second hand smoke (ETS) is a proven health danger.* The
Environmental Protection Agency (EPA) report naming Environmental
Tobacco Smoke (ETS) as a class A carcinogen is a triumph of politics over
science, and a symbol of corruption of science by government. The Congressional Research Service of the Library of Congress demolished their
conclusions.

• *It is false that tobacco is more dangerous than drugs or alcohol.* The CDC
inflates the deaths from tobacco, and ignores the fact that tobacco is not
an intoxicant, and alcohol and drugs are. Intoxicants destroy physical co-
ordination, emotional restraint, and moral standards. Alcohol and drug
abuse contribute to crime, violence, spouse abuse, child neglect, sexual
promiscuity and sexually transmitted diseases. Nicotine does none of
these things.

• *It is false that smokers are a financial burden to society.* Economists,
with rare unanimity, have shown that smokers are not a net cost to the
government, but a saving. Smokers pay heavy cigarette taxes, and also,
because their life expectancy is somewhat less than non-smokers (by
about three to five years), they collect less in social security, pensions,
Medicare, and Medicaid. A complete report on these economic matters
was issued by the Congressional Research Service of the Library of Congress in March 1994.

• *It is false that smoking has no health benefits at all.* Smokers are less
obese than non-smokers, and since obesity is a risk factor for heart disease, diabetes, and stroke, preventing obesity should count as a benefit in
health reckoning. Nicotine also has an anti-depressant, anti-anxiety effect, improves alertness, attention, and concentration. There is increasing
evidence that smoking tends to reduce incidence of Alzheimer's and
Parkinson's diseases, and to ameliorate the symptoms of schizophrenia.
But scientists in these fields have a great deal of trouble getting funding,
because of ASP opposition to any good word for tobacco.

The corruption of science

How have the ASPs managed to convince the American people that these
falsehoods are true? They used Big Lie Technique (Hitler's favorite), that
people will believe anything if leaders repeat it often enough. They used
mountains of junk statistics, which are difficult to understand by the
laypeople, and easy to manipulate by "experts." And worst of all, they
mercilessly suppressed criticism by honest scientists, whom they branded

as dishonest tools of the tobacco companies. Theodor Sterling, a fellow of the American College of Epidemiology, wrote a tongue-in-cheek piece showing that the CDC method could be used to prove that *not smoking* caused 270,000 deaths a year. He wrote a serious paper showing that by use of only two honest corrections to the CDC work, the number of purported smoking deaths could be cut in half. Sterling was blasted by the ASP guru Stanton Glantz, whose economic work has recently been demolished by the economist Michael Evans.

The Federal Health establishment, controlling a vast portion of biomedical research money, has the power to deny grants and end the careers of scientists who oppose the ASPs' corruption of science. In fact, censorship has gone so far that many American journals will not publish or even review papers by authors who receive any money from tobacco interests!

By vastly overrating the dangers of tobacco, and neglecting those of alcohol and drugs, the Anti-Smoking Police (ASPs) have gravely distorted the proper priorities for our resources.

The politicization of science, treated by David Tell ("Pack of Lies," *Weekly Standard*, June 16, 1997) and by me in a letter to the *Standard* (July 7, 1997), is not the only offense of the War on Smoking. The tactics of the attorneys-general against the tobacco companies are a serious abuse of government power. [In the 1990s, dozens of states sued the tobacco industry to recover the health-care costs of treating illnesses claimed to be caused by smoking. A settlement was reached in 1998.] Read Michael Kelly's scathing *New Republic* editorial ("TRB from Washington: Take Your Medicine," July 14–21, 1997). Robert J. Samuelson (*Washington Post*, Op-Ed, July 2, 1997) showed how a group of private attorneys planned, financed, and directed the suit, which will earn billions for them—"How they hijacked the public policy for private enrichment is the little-told story of the tobacco settlement." The increased cigarette taxes are regressive and unfair. Paul Gigot, in the *Wall Street Journal* (Op-Ed, June 27, 1997) revealed that Hugh Rodham, President Bill Clinton's brother-in-law, and Richard Scruggs, Republican senator Trent Lott's brother-in-law, are members of the greedy lawyers' group.

The War on Smoking, which started with a germ of truth—that smoking is a high risk factor for lung cancer—has grown into a monster of deceit, tyranny, and greed, further eroding the credibility of the government, and harming our health and welfare. The true dangers to our society are crime, violence, family breakdown, and out-of-wedlock births, none of which arises from smoking, but from alcohol and drug abuse, lack of moral values, and poverty.

Nicotine Is an Addictive Substance

Alan I. Leshner

Alan I. Leshner is the director of the National Institute on Drug Abuse.

Nicotine, an active ingredient in tobacco, is extremely addictive. It operates by elevating levels of the neurotransmitter dopamine, a pleasure-inducing brain chemical. Although various nicotine-replacement therapies and some medications can successfully treat nicotine addiction, most smokers still have difficulty quitting. The public health community must continue to address the problem of cigarette smoking by combining pharmacological treatments with behavioral therapies, by identifying risk factors for drug addiction, and by increasing preventative efforts.

Editor's Note: This viewpoint was originally a prepared statement presented to a Senate committee during its hearings on tobacco control legislation on February 10, 1998.

Mr. Chairman and Members of the Committee, I am pleased to be here with my distinguished colleagues to discuss current research findings and future research directions on one of the Nation's deadliest and most costly health problems—use of tobacco products. It is addiction to nicotine that is at the root of this enormous burden.

An addictive drug

Scientific research has determined that nicotine is in fact a highly addictive drug. Nicotine addiction, like other drug addictions, is characterized by compulsive drug seeking and use, even in the face of negative health consequences. A testimony to this fact is that most smokers identify smoking as harmful and nearly 35 million of them attempt to quit each year. Yet only a very small fraction of them actually succeed.

Emerging basic research is reinforcing what earlier studies have indi-

Reprinted from Alan I. Leshner, testimony before the U.S. Senate Hearings of the Committee on Labor and Human Resources, 105th Cong., 2nd sess., part 4, February 10, 1998.

cated about the highly addictive nature of nicotine. Let me share with you a sampling of some of our most recent and interesting research findings.

Recently we have been able to prove what has been only inferred from earlier research, that some of nicotine's most important effects are exerted through the very same brain circuits as those of other drugs of abuse. Researchers found nicotine, just like cocaine, heroin and marijuana, activates dopamine containing neurons in the critical brain pathways that control reward and pleasure. This finding supports a convergence of data pointing toward at least one major commonality among all drugs of abuse: they all elevate levels of the neurotransmitter dopamine. It is this change in dopamine that is believed to be a fundamental root of all addictions.

Scientific research has determined that nicotine is in fact a highly addictive drug.

Another new and exciting finding published [in 1998], scientists pinpointed a particular protein, the beta 2 subunit of the nicotinic cholinergic receptor, as being essential to the process of nicotine addiction. Using sophisticated bioengineering tools, these researchers produced a new strain of knockout mice which lack this important protein. Mice without this receptor would not self administer nicotine, whereas those who had the receptor readily sought to give themselves nicotine infusions. This clearly demonstrates that this beta 2 subunit is an important mediator of nicotine's addictive properties.

Nicotine may not be the only psychoactive ingredient in tobacco, however. Using advanced neuroimaging (PET) technology we are now actually able to see what tobacco smoking is doing to the brain of an awake and behaving human being. One dramatic effect that cigarette smoking has on the brain [is] a tremendous decrease in the levels of an important enzyme known to be responsible for breaking down dopamine, called monoamineoxidase-B (MAO-B). The net effect of this reduction in MAO-B is an increase in dopamine levels. Importantly, this particular effect is not caused by nicotine but by some additional unknown compound in cigarette smoke. Nicotine itself does not alter MAO-B levels; it affects dopamine through other mechanisms. Thus there may be multiple routes by which smoking alters the neurotransmitter dopamine, and, again, this neurochemical is centrally implicated in the effects of all addictive substances.

Through studies like this we are unraveling the mysteries of not only smoking as an addiction, but these findings are giving us new information that may be relevant to other addictions as well.

Treating cigarette addiction

Through NIDA's [National Institute on Drug Abuse] leadership, the world now has a variety of effective pharmacological and behavioral treatments to select from to help people conquer their smoking addiction, but we need more. Addiction researchers have developed a number of new pharmacological weapons to combat nicotine addiction. For example, several nicotine-replacement therapies, including the patch and gum, are now readily available in local drug stores and supermarkets. In addition, our scientists are working on a number of non-nicotine replacement therapies as well. The preeminent compound in this line is Buproprion, which you may know as Zyban®. Originally marketed as Welbutrin®, an antidepressant, this compound is showing promising results in treating nicotine addiction as well.

While we have a number of treatments that have proven to be effective for many people, we still do not have enough in our clinical toolbox. NIDA will continue to build upon its basic addiction research portfolio to identify and develop innovative approaches to treat nicotine addiction.

Of course, recognizing that smoking is a complex behavioral as well as a pharmacological problem, it needs to be approached as such. Thus behavioral interventions play an integral role in nicotine addiction treatment. To further improve the efficacy of these combined approaches, we must better understand the antecedents of tobacco use, and learn how to change behavior patterns. Both research and extensive clinical experiences have taught us that treating the addiction with just medications is not nearly as effective as when we couple the medication with a behavioral approach.

We know that more than 90 percent of the people who try to quit smoking relapse or return to smoking within one year. The majority of them relapse within a week. There are, however, two-and-a-half to five percent who do in fact succeed on their own. It has been shown that pharmacological treatments can double the odds of their success. However, a combination of pharmacological and behavioral treatments can even further improve their odds. For example, when use of the nicotine patch is combined with a behavioral approach, such as group therapy or social support networks, the efficacy of treatment is enhanced.

Prevention efforts

Just as with other drugs, ultimately our best treatment is prevention. Twenty years of prevention research has given us the tools that we need to develop effective programs to prevent people from beginning to smoke, even young people.

This holds for other drugs of abuse as well. The time of common sense approaches and intuition in preventing drug use is over. We have a science base for prevention and we need to use it. Toward this end, NIDA has produced the first ever research-based guide for preventing drug use. The very same principles espoused in the book, *Preventing Drug Use Among Children and Adolescents*, hold for all drugs of abuse, including nicotine. These principles can be applied by families, schools and communities to ensure the health and well being of future generations.

We are not stopping here, however. We are forging ahead to identify risk factors that may make an individual more vulnerable to addiction. Understanding what makes a person vulnerable, and how they progress from their first drug exposure to abusing drugs to addiction, will enable us to effectively target our prevention efforts to those who are most at risk. Just as important, however, is the identification of protective factors, those behaviors, environments, activities, etc. that seem to enable a person to avoid drug use altogether. Both risk and protective factors may be genetic, biological, environmental, social or cultural in nature, for nicotine, as well as for all other addictive drugs.

It is only through the recognition of tobacco use as an addiction that we will be able to eliminate many of its detrimental health effects. As with all other disorders, it is research on addiction that provides hope for even more effective prevention and treatment approaches.

The President [Bill Clinton] stressed that the following five key elements must be at the heart of any national tobacco legislation: (1) A comprehensive plan to reduce teen smoking, including a combination of penalties and price increases that raise cigarette prices up to $1.50 per pack over the next 10 years as necessary to meet youth smoking targets; (2) Express reaffirmation that the Food and Drug Administration has full authority to regulate tobacco products; (3) Changes in the way the tobacco industry does business; (4) Progress toward other critical public health goals, such as the expansion of smoking cessation and prevention programs and the reduction of secondhand smoke; and (5) Protection for tobacco farmers and their communities.

Never before has the momentum for addressing this public health crisis been greater. There are tremendous scientific opportunities, based on at least two decades of scientific accomplishments. We must seize the scientific opportunities that now present themselves to ensure that no more lives are lost to what is ultimately both a preventable and, if not prevented, a treatable disease.

5

Smokers Are Not Necessarily Addicted to Nicotine

Richard J. DeGrandpre

Richard J. DeGrandpre, an independent scholar of drugs and culture, is coeditor of Drug Policy and Human Nature *and coauthor of* The Changeable Self.

Nicotine dependency is not necessarily the reason that some people acquire a cigarette smoking habit. The fact that only a minority of smokers who attempt to quit have success with nicotine-replacement therapy suggests that nonchemical or environmental factors may trigger the desire to smoke. Public health advocates who insist that nicotine is the addictive agent in cigarettes only exacerbate the problem by leading smokers to believe that they are enslaved by a drug. A fuller understanding of the varieties of addiction is needed to help curb cigarette addiction.

During the 1996 presidential election campaign, Bill Clinton successfully cast Big Tobacco as a national enemy, with Bob Dole playing the role of collaborator by downplaying the addictiveness of nicotine. Meanwhile, the Food and Drug Administration has been asserting jurisdiction over cigarettes as "nicotine delivery devices," arguing that tobacco companies intend to hook their customers, just like schoolyard drug pushers. Hundreds of pending lawsuits, including class actions and cases filed by state governments, similarly allege a conspiracy to addict smokers. These developments represent important changes in our attitudes toward cigarettes. Though justified in the name of public health, the increasing emphasis on the enslaving power of nicotine may only make matters worse.

The classical model of addiction

Understanding why requires careful consideration of the conventional wisdom about tobacco addiction, which recycles mistaken assumptions about illicit drugs. During the latter half of the twentieth century, the classical model of addiction, derived from observations of narcotic abuse, increasingly has been used to describe the cigarette habit. The classical model states that consumption of certain chemicals causes a physical dependence, either immediately or after prolonged use, characterized by withdrawal symptoms—symptoms that can be avoided or escaped only by further drug use. As Steven Hyman, director of the National Institute of Mental Health [NIMH], opined recently in *Science*, "Repeated doses of addictive drugs—opiates, cocaine, and amphetamine—cause drug dependence and, afterward, withdrawal."

If nicotine is so relentlessly addictive, how can it be that 50 percent of all Americans who have ever smoked no longer do?

This cyclical model, in which the drug serves as both problem and solution, offers a simple, easy-to-grasp account of the addiction process, giving the concept great staying power in the public imagination. In the case of smoking, this view of addiction is central to the rationale for regulating tobacco and the concern that the cigarette companies have been doping their products with extra nicotine. But the classical model tends to conceal rather than elucidate the ultimate sources of addiction, and it is just as ill-suited to the cigarette habit as it has always been for understanding illicit drug use.

If a chemical compound can be addictive in the manner described by NIMH Director Hyman, we would expect anyone who regularly uses such a substance to become addicted. Yet only a minority of those who use illicit drugs—whether marijuana, cocaine, or heroin—ever develop a dependence on them. The prevalence of addiction, as defined by the American Psychiatric Association's *Diagnostic and Statistical Manual*, among users of alcohol and cocaine runs about 15 percent and 17 percent, respectively. Even in a sample of 79 regular crack users, Patricia Erickson and her colleagues at Toronto's Addiction Research Foundation found that only about 37 percent used the drug heavily (more than 100 times in their lives), and 67 percent had not used in the past month. A similar pattern holds for tobacco. In the 1994 National Household Survey on Drug Abuse, 73 percent of respondents reported smoking cigarettes at some time, but only about 29 percent reported smoking in the previous month, and not necessarily on a daily basis. Writing in the May/June 1996 *Mother Jones*, Jeffrey Klein manages to argue that nicotine enslaves its users and, at the same time, that Tobacco Inc. seeks to recruit young smokers to replace the 1.3 million Americans who quit each year. If nicotine is so relentlessly addictive, how can it be that 50 percent of all Americans who have ever smoked no longer do?

The classical model also suggests that the cigarette habit should be highly amenable to nicotine replacement therapy, such as the nicotine patch. Yet few of the tens of thousands of patch users have actually broken the habit (only about 10 percent to 15 percent succeed). In direct conflict with the classical model, most keep smoking while on the patch, continuing to consume the carcinogens in cigarette smoke while obtaining considerably higher blood levels of nicotine. A 1992 study of nicotine replacement therapy reported in the journal *Psychopharmacology* concluded that the "overall lack of effect [of the patch] on cigarette consumption is perhaps surprising and suggests that in regular smokers the lighting up of a cigarette is generally triggered by cues other than low plasma nicotine levels."

Most people who successfully quit smoking do so only after several failed attempts. If addiction is driven by physical dependence on a chemical—in this case, nicotine—relapse should occur during withdrawal, which for nicotine typically lasts a few weeks. Yet a sizable proportion of relapses occur long after the smoker has suffered through nicotine withdrawal. In fact, studies do not even show a relationship between the severity of withdrawal and the likelihood of relapse. As any former smoker could tell you, ex-smokers crave cigarettes at certain times and in certain situations for months, even years, after quitting. In these cases, the desire to smoke is triggered by environmental cues, not by withdrawal symptoms. This is one reason why people who overcome addiction to illicit substances such as heroin or cocaine often say they had more difficulty breaking the cigarette habit. Because regular tobacco users smoke in a wide array of circumstances (when bored, after eating, when driving) and settings (home, work, car), the cues that elicit the urge are more ubiquitous than for illicit drug use.

These failures of the classical model illustrate how conventional wisdom over-simplifies the dynamics of cigarette smoking. This reductionist view is dangerous because it ignores the psychosocial factors that underlie addiction. In coming to terms with cigarette addiction as a psychosocial process, rather than a simple pharmacological one, we need to distinguish between cigarette addiction and nicotine addiction. Certainly no one (except perhaps the tobacco companies) denies that cigarette smoking can be addictive, if by addiction one means a stubborn urge to keep smoking. But it is quite a different matter to say that nicotine accounts for the addictiveness of smoking. Nicotine withdrawal notwithstanding, nicotine alone is insufficient, and may even be unnecessary, to create cigarette addiction.

Addictions are not always drug-related

This claim can be clarified by two dramatic case studies reported in the *British Journal of Addiction* in 1973 and 1989. The earlier article described a 47-year-old woman with a two-and-a-half-year-long dependence on *water*, one of several such cases noted by the author. The woman reported a nagging withdrawal symptom—a dry, salty taste in her mouth—that was alleviated by the persistent drinking of water (up to 60 glasses per day). This case of dependence on a nonpsychoactive substance contrasts sharply with the second account, which described an 80-year-old woman who used cocaine without incident for 55 years. The authors reported that "she denies any feelings of euphoria or increased energy after [snorting] the cocaine nor any depression or craving for cocaine when her supplies run out. . . . She appears to have suffered no ill effects from the prolonged use of cocaine in physical, psychological or social terms." So we see that not every addiction involves drug use and not every instance of drug use involves an addiction.

To say that cigarette addiction is a psychosocial process means that social, cultural, and economic factors play a crucial role in acquiring and keeping a cigarette habit. In fact, the tendency to reduce the cigarette experience to chemical servitude may be one of the most powerful cultural factors driving addiction. Cigarette lore wrongly teaches smokers (and smokers-to-be) that they will suffer badly if they attempt to quit, while at the same time freeing them of responsibility for their drug use once they begin. Such beliefs also help romanticize cigarette smoking, elevating nicotine to a sublime abstraction. This not only reinforces the forbidden fruit effect, it helps transform the habit of smoking into a cult behavior. Smoking thus acquires the kind of meaning that the youth of America are most in search of: social meaning. As Richard Klein writes in *Cigarettes Are Sublime*, "smoking cigarettes is not only a physical act but a discursive one—a wordless but eloquent form of expression."

Nicotine alone is insufficient, and may even be unnecessary, to create cigarette addiction.

To counteract the forces that give momentum to drug use, the public meaning of addiction needs to be broadened to include the many, changing facets of the psychosocial realm in which we develop. "Putting people back in charge" of their addictions, as John Leo puts it in *U.S. News & World Report*, will not work if we focus only on the naked individual. Rather than pushing the pendulum of public policy between scapegoating the substance and scapegoating the individual, we should seek a middle ground. Realizing that the addiction process has at least three levels of complexity is a good place to start.

First, at the basic and most immediate level, are the short- and long-term biological processes that underlie the psychological experiences of drug use and drug abstinence. Even with the same drug, these experiences vary greatly across individuals. Scientists and journalists too easily forget that every psychological process is built on biology. Discoveries of biological mechanisms and processes underlying addiction are not proof that the problem is biological rather than social and psychological. Eating rich foods has powerful biological effects in both the short and long run, but we should not therefore conclude that the rise in obesity in the United States is a biological problem. Indeed, attempts to alter the addiction process that emphasize biochemistry (such as the nicotine patch) have met with little success.

At the next level are psychological processes (social, motivational, learning) that, although rooted in biology, are shaped by personal experience. Because each of us has unique life experiences, we do not necessarily interpret the same events in the same way. The reasons for one individual's addiction may be altogether different from the reasons for another's. As the 1996 Scottish film *Trainspotting* makes clear, stories of addiction are no less complex than any other personal stories. Still, intervention at this level has had some success with users of alcohol or illicit drugs, and several research and treatment institutions are examining methods for "matching" addicts with different treatment strategies based on their social and psychological characteristics.

Drug effects and drug addiction also vary greatly across time and place, implicating cultural factors as the third and most general aspect of drug addiction. These factors are rooted in but not reducible to psychological processes, just as psychological processes are not reducible to biology. Patterns of alcohol use around the world, which show that the prevalence of drinking problems cannot be predicted by consumption alone, illustrate the importance of culture. Italians, for example, historically have consumed large quantities of alcohol with relatively low rates of drunkenness and alcoholism. The effects of alcohol on human behavior—violence, boorishness, gregariousness—also have been shown to vary dramatically across cultures.

Given the cultural role in addiction and the radical changes that have occurred in attitudes about smoking, it is quite possible that the young smokers of today are not at all like the smokers of 50 years ago. Those who begin smoking now do so with the belief that it is addictive, causes poor health (and wrinkles!), and can be deadly. If individuals are willing to start smoking despite such knowledge, it is likely that they will acquire and keep the habit, seeming to confirm the current, politically correct image of addiction. And if this self-fulfilling prophecy is realized, chances are that interventions aimed at the social realm will continue to miss their target and fail to curtail addiction.

Secondhand Smoke Endangers Human Health

United States Environmental Protection Agency

The Environmental Protection Agency (EPA), created in 1970, is the federal agency in charge of controlling and preventing air and water pollution caused by contaminants and toxins. EPA headquarters are in Washington, D.C.

Secondhand smoke, also known as environmental tobacco smoke or ETS, is harmful to human health. Considerable evidence drawn from scientific investigations and epidemiology studies proves that secondhand smoke can cause respiratory illnesses and lung cancer in nonsmokers. Critics of these findings contend that the Environmental Protection Agency has manipulated data to arrive at a predetermined conclusion, and that no studies have definitively confirmed a causal relationship between secondhand smoke and cancer. However, all of the epidemiology studies reveal that people who have longer-term exposure to secondhand smoke face an increased risk of developing lung cancer.

In early 1993, the United States Environmental Protection Agency (EPA) released a report *(Respiratory Health Effects of Passive Smoking: Lung Cancer and Other Disorders;* EPA/600/6-90/006 F) that evaluated the respiratory health effects from breathing secondhand smoke (also called environmental tobacco smoke). In that report, EPA concluded that secondhand smoke causes lung cancer in adult nonsmokers and impairs the respiratory health of children. These findings are very similar to ones made previously by the National Academy of Sciences and the U.S. Surgeon General.

The EPA report classified secondhand smoke as a Group A carcinogen, a designation which means that there is sufficient evidence that the substance causes cancer in humans. The Group A designation has been used by EPA for only 15 other pollutants, including asbestos, radon, and benzene. Only secondhand smoke has actually been shown in studies to cause cancer at typical environmental levels. EPA estimates that approxi-

Reprinted from *Setting the Record Straight: Secondhand Smoke Is a Preventable Health Risk,* a publication of the U.S. Environmental Protection Agency, June 1994, number EPA 402-F-94-005.

mately 3,000 American nonsmokers die each year from lung cancer caused by secondhand smoke.

Every year, an estimated 150,000 to 300,000 children under 18 months of age get pneumonia or bronchitis from breathing secondhand tobacco smoke. Secondhand smoke is a risk factor for the development of asthma in children and worsens the condition of up to one million asthmatic children.

EPA has clear authority to inform the public about indoor air pollution health risks and what can be done to reduce those risks. EPA has a particular responsibility to do everything possible to warn of risks to the health of children.

A recent high profile advertising and public relations campaign by the tobacco industry may confuse the American public about the risks of secondhand smoke. EPA believes it's time to set the record straight about an indisputable fact: secondhand smoke is a real and preventable health risk.

EPA absolutely stands by its scientific and well documented report. The report was the subject of an extensive open review both by the public and by EPA's Science Advisory Board (SAB), a panel of independent scientific experts. Virtually every one of the arguments about lung cancer advanced by the tobacco industry and its consultants was addressed by the SAB. The panel concurred in the methodology and unanimously endorsed the conclusions of the final report.

The report has also been endorsed by the U.S. Department of Health and Human Services, the National Cancer Institute, the Surgeon General, and many major health organizations.

Classification of secondhand smoke as a carcinogen

The finding that secondhand smoke causes lung cancer in nonsmoking adults is based on the total weight of the available evidence and is not dependent on any single analysis. This evidence includes several important facts.

First, it is indisputable that smoking tobacco causes lung cancer in humans, and there is no evidence that there is a threshold below which smoking will not cause cancer.

Second, although secondhand smoke is a dilute mixture of "mainstream" smoke exhaled by smokers and "sidestream" smoke from the burning end of a cigarette or other tobacco product, it is chemically similar to the smoke inhaled by smokers, and contains a number of carcinogenic compounds.

Third, there is considerable evidence that large numbers of people who do not smoke are exposed to, absorb, and metabolize significant amounts of secondhand smoke.

Fourth, there is supporting evidence from laboratory studies of the ability of secondhand smoke both to cause cancer in animals and to damage DNA, which is recognized by scientists as being an instrumental mechanism in cancer development.

Finally, EPA conducted multiple analyses on the then-available 30 epidemiology studies from eight different countries which examined the association between secondhand smoke and lung cancer in women who never smoked themselves but were exposed to their husband's smoke.

Since the epidemiology studies are the major thrust of the tobacco industry arguments against the EPA report, these studies are examined in more detail below.

The epidemiology studies

The most important aspect of the review of the epidemiology studies is the remarkable consistency of results across studies that support a causal association between secondhand smoke and lung cancer.

In assessing the studies several different ways, it becomes clear that the extent of the consistency defies attribution to chance. When looking only at the simple measure of exposure of whether the husband ever smoked, 24 of 30 studies reported an increase in risk for nonsmoking women with smoking husbands. Since many of these studies were small, the chance of declaring these increases statistically significant was small. Still, nine of these were statistically significant, and the probability that this many of the studies would be statistically significant merely by chance is less than *1 in 10 thousand*.

The simple overall comparison of risks in ever vs. never exposed to spousal smoking tends to hide true increases in risk in two ways. First, it categorizes many women as never exposed who actually received exposure from sources other than spousal smoking. It also includes some women as exposed who actually received little exposure from their husband's smoking. One way to correct for this latter case is to look at the women whose husbands smoked the most. When one looks at the 17 studies that examined cancer effects based on the *level* of exposure of the subjects, *every* study found an increased lung cancer risk among those subjects who were most exposed. Nine were statistically significant. The probability of 9 out of 17 studies showing statistically significant results occurring by chance is less than *1 in ten million*.

Probably the most important finding for a causal relationship is one of increasing response with increasing exposure, since such associations cannot usually be explained by other factors. Such exposure-response trends were seen in *all* 14 studies that examined the relationship between level of exposure and effect. In 10 of the studies the trends were statistically significant. The probability of this happening by chance is less than *1 in a billion*.

Secondhand smoke causes lung cancer in adult nonsmokers and impairs the respiratory health of children.

It is unprecedented for such a consistency of results to be seen in epidemiology studies of cancer from environmental levels of a pollutant. One reason is that it is extremely difficult to detect an effect when virtually everyone is exposed, as is the case with secondhand smoke. However, consistent increased risks for those most exposed and consistent trends of increasing exposure showing an increasing effect provide strong evidence that secondhand smoke increases the risk of lung cancer in nonsmokers.

The evidence is clear and consistent: secondhand smoke is a cause of lung cancer in adults who don't smoke. EPA has never claimed that minimal exposure to secondhand smoke poses a huge individual cancer risk. Even though the lung cancer risk from secondhand smoke is relatively small compared to the risk from direct smoking, unlike a smoker who chooses to smoke, the nonsmoker's risk is often involuntary. In addition, exposure to secondhand smoke varies tremendously among exposed individuals. For those who must live or work in close proximity to one or more smokers, the risk would certainly be greater than for those less exposed.

EPA estimates that secondhand smoke is responsible for about 3,000 lung cancer deaths each year among nonsmokers in the U.S.; of these, the estimate is 800 from exposure to secondhand smoke at home and 2,200 from exposure in work or social situations.

The risks to children are widely acknowledged

The conclusion that secondhand smoke causes respiratory effects in children is widely shared and virtually undisputed. Even the tobacco industry does not contest these effects in its media and public relations campaign.

EPA estimates that every year, between 150,000 and 300,000 children under 1-1/2 years of age get bronchitis or pneumonia from breathing secondhand tobacco smoke, resulting in thousands of hospitalizations. In children under 18 years of age, secondhand smoke exposure also results in more coughing and wheezing, a small but significant decrease in lung function, and an increase in fluid in the middle ear. Children with asthma have more frequent and more severe asthma attacks because of exposure to secondhand smoke, which is also a risk factor for the onset of asthma in children who did not previously have symptoms.

Secondhand smoke contains strong irritants and sensitizers and many adults, as well as children, suffer irritation and other acute effects whenever they are exposed to secondhand smoke. In addition, there is mounting evidence that exposure to secondhand smoke can have an effect on the cardiovascular system, although the EPA report does not address this issue.

A response to criticisms of EPA findings

The tobacco industry is raising numerous issues which may distract the public from the fact that secondhand smoke poses a real and preventable health risk. The tobacco industry neither acknowledges nor disputes EPA's conclusions of respiratory effects in children. It focuses instead on EPA's findings on lung cancer.

The overall thrusts of the tobacco industry's arguments are that EPA manipulated the lung cancer data to come to a predetermined conclusion. The industry also argues that a nonsmoker's exposure to secondhand smoke is so small as to be insignificant. The argument on minimal exposure is belied both by the acute irritation and respiratory effects and the fallacy of the "cigarette equivalents" approach discussed below. Responses to the specific criticisms of EPA's assessment of the lung cancer data follow.

• *The 11 U.S. lung cancer studies.* Critics of the EPA report argue that by normal statistical standards, none of the 11 U.S. studies included in the EPA report showed a statistically significant increase in the simple overall risk measure, and that EPA should therefore have been unable to conclude that secondhand smoke causes lung cancer in nonsmokers. These critics are misrepresenting a small part of the total evidence on secondhand smoke and lung cancer.

The consistency of study results in the highest exposure category and exposure-response trends discussed above also apply to the U.S. studies. For example, seven of the 11 U.S. studies had fewer than 45 cases, making statistical comparisons difficult. Nonetheless, eight of the 11 had increased overall risks, and for the seven studies which reported on risks by amount of exposure, the highest exposure groups in *all* seven had increased risks. While the 11 U.S. studies are not, by themselves, conclusive, they do support the conclusion that secondhand smoke is causally associated with lung cancer.

• *Studies completed since release of the EPA report.* Critics claim that had EPA not "excluded" the recent R.C. Brownson study, the Agency could not have concluded that secondhand smoke causes cancer. In fact, four new lung cancer epidemiology studies, including the Brownson study, have been published since the literature review cutoff date for the 1993 EPA report, and *all* support EPA's conclusions. Three of these are large U.S. studies funded, at least in part, by the National Cancer Institute. A 1992 study of Florida women by H.G. Stockwell et al. found a 60% overall increased risk of lung cancer from exposure to their husband's smoke, with significant results for both the highest exposure group and the exposure-response trend. The 1992 study of Missouri women by Brownson et al. found no overall increased risk, but did demonstrate a significant increase in risk in the highest spousal smoking exposure group and a positive exposure-response trend.

Secondhand smoke is a real and preventable health risk.

The 1994 study by Elizabeth Fontham et al. of women in two California and three Southern cities is the largest case-control study on the subject ever conducted and is considered by EPA to be the best designed study on secondhand smoke and lung cancer conducted to date. This study found significantly increased risks for overall exposure and in the highest exposure group and a strong positive exposure-response relationship. These findings were significant not only for exposure from spouses, but also for exposure in the workplace and in social situations.

• *90% vs. 95% confidence intervals.* Critics of the EPA report have charged that EPA changed the confidence interval in order to come to a predetermined conclusion. However, the conclusion that secondhand smoke is a known human carcinogen simply does not hinge on whether or not a 95% or 90% "confidence interval" was used. A confidence interval is used to display variability in relative risk estimates in the epidemiology studies. As discussed above, the Group A designation is based on the total weight of the available evidence. The consistency of results that are seen in the numerous studies examined lead to a certainty of greater than 99.9% that secondhand smoke increases the risk of lung cancer in nonsmokers.

Use of what is called in statistics a "one-tailed test of significance," which often corresponds to a 90% confidence interval, is a standard and appropriate statistical procedure in certain circumstances. The "one-tailed test" is used when there is prior evidence that if there is an effect from a substance, it is highly likely to be an adverse rather than a protective effect, or vice versa. In the case of secondhand smoke, an extensive database exists for direct smoking indicating that if chemically similar secondhand smoke also has a lung cancer effect, this effect is likely to be similarly adverse. EPA used one-tailed significance tests for lung cancer in both external drafts of the risk assessment document as well as the final report. Ninety percent confidence intervals were also used in other EPA cancer risk assessments, including methylene chloride, coke oven emissions, radon, nickel, and dioxin.

Secondhand smoke is responsible for about 3000 lung cancer deaths each year among nonsmokers in the U.S.

In the non-cancer respiratory effects portions of the report, "two-tailed tests" and 95% confidence intervals were used, since there was less prior evidence from smokers to suggest that secondhand smoke would cause bronchitis, pneumonia, and ear infections in children.

• *The meta-analysis.* Meta-analysis was used for the lung cancer data as an objective method of combining results from many studies and was specifically endorsed by the SAB for use with this database. Some critics argue both that the meta-analysis was not an appropriate technique, and that had EPA included the Brownson study (addressed above) in the meta-analysis of overall spousal exposure, EPA could not possibly have classified secondhand smoke as a known human carcinogen. This just isn't true.

The finding that secondhand smoke is a known cause of lung cancer in humans is based on all the evidence and is not dependent on the meta-analysis of the simple ever- vs. never-exposed comparisons, as the critics suggest. If the meta-analysis were removed from the report entirely, the findings would be precisely the same. The meta-analysis was used primarily for estimating and quantifying the population risks from exposure to secondhand smoke, and an alternative approach also used in the report gave very similar results.

• *Confounders.* In the secondhand smoke report, a confounder would be a specific factor that could be responsible for the lung cancer increases observed in nonsmokers instead of secondhand smoke. The tobacco industry and its consultants have suggested, for example, that nonsmoking wives might share in the same poor dietary habits as their smoking husbands, increasing their risk.

The consistency of results across different countries where lifestyle factors, including diet, vary, argues against confounding. For example, while the tobacco industry theorizes that a high fat diet is a confounding factor, the studies from Japan, where dietary fat intake is among the lowest in the world, show a strong dose-response relationship for secondhand smoke and lung cancer.

The EPA report did examine the available data for six potential confounders such as occupation, dietary factors, and history of lung disease, and concluded that none was likely to explain the lung cancer increases seen in the studies.

The 1994 Fontham et al. study controlled for diet and other potential confounders, and concluded, "These observations indicate that the strong association in this study between adult secondhand smoke exposure and lung cancer risk cannot be attributed to any likely confounder."

• *The "threshold theory."* Although some have argued that tobacco smoke cannot cause cancer below a certain level, there is no evidence that this threshold exists. In the absence of such evidence, carcinogens at any level are considered by EPA to increase risk somewhat, although the degree of risk certainly is reduced as exposure decreases. The increased risks observed in the secondhand smoke epidemiology studies are further evidence that any threshold for secondhand smoke would have to be at very low levels.

• *"Cigarette equivalents."* The tobacco industry uses the "cigarette equivalent" method of comparing smokers' and nonsmokers' exposures to a single component of tobacco smoke to infer that a nonsmoker's exposure to tobacco smoke is insignificant. However, the cigarette equivalent method has no scientific support, and was rejected by the SAB panel that reviewed the EPA report. Among the many problems with this method is the fact that while secondhand smoke and mainstream smoke contain the same approximately 4,000 compounds, their ratios of individual compounds differ by factors in the thousands. Thus, there is no single compound in tobacco smoke that is an adequate indicator for drawing such comparisons. An RJ Reynolds newspaper ad, while utilizing the method, acknowledges it may not be relevant for assessing risk from secondhand smoke.

• *Residential exposures translated to the workplace.* The tobacco industry frequently argues that because most studies were based on residential exposures, secondhand smoke has not been shown to be a hazard in the workplace. A substance capable of causing cancer in one environment is certainly capable of causing it in any other environment where exposures are comparable, as is the case with residential and workplace exposure to secondhand smoke. In fact, the 1994 Fontham study found a slightly higher risk for workplace exposure than for residential exposures.

Having a choice to take a risk for themselves should not permit smokers to impose a risk on others.

• *The Congressional Research Service (CRS) report.* The RJ Reynolds' media campaign cites a report prepared by the Congressional Research Service (CRS) on cigarette taxes to fund health care reform to argue that CRS believes that the epidemiological evidence on secondhand smoke and health effects is "weak and uncertain." However, CRS has not taken a position on either EPA's risk assessment or the health effects of passive smoking.

Two economists from CRS, citing material largely prepared by the tobacco industry, included a discussion of EPA's risk assessment in an economic analysis of a cigarette excise tax proposal to fund health care reform. In EPA's view, the CRS economists' cursory look at the issues is not comparable to the exhaustive analyses and rigorous review process which EPA undertook when examining the extensive database on secondhand smoke and respiratory health. EPA is confident that a comprehensive analysis of the secondhand smoke database by expert scientists from CRS, with adequate peer review, will come to conclusions about the risks of secondhand smoke similar to those of EPA and many other organizations.

Cigarette prohibition?

The claim that the government is attempting to bring back prohibition—this time for cigarettes—is a complete fabrication and utter nonsense. EPA's interest is to provide information to protect the nonsmoker from involuntary exposure to a hazardous substance. Having a choice to take a risk for themselves should not permit smokers to impose a risk on others.

7

The Dangers of Secondhand Smoke Are Negligible

Sarah Mahler-Vossler

Sarah Mahler-Vossler has a doctorate in business from the City University of New York and has been an associate professor of management at Hartwick College in Oneonta, New York.

No conclusive evidence proves that secondhand smoke (also known as environmental tobacco smoke or ETS) significantly increases the risk for respiratory illnesses and heart disease among nonsmokers. The highly publicized reports on the alleged dangers of secondhand smoke are based on faulty studies and mishandled statistics. Policy makers, government agencies, and public health officials—motivated by the current smoking prohibitionist fervor—cite the few studies that back up their own foregone conclusions about ETS and ignore those revealing that the dangers of secondhand smoke are negligible.

It's a lot easier to scare people than it is to *unscare* them. When guilt is added to fear, the task is even tougher. Americans have been convinced that environmental tobacco smoke, or ETS, is dangerous. Of course they're frightened, and smokers have been made to feel guilty. They fear they are hurting, maybe killing others—maybe even their own children. Media-mediated and neighbor-reinforced, this scary message about ETS gets an even wetter Pavlovian slaver when the alarm-bell ringers are top government officials or those with names followed by lots of letters and fancy affiliations. But these highly publicized claims from seemingly trustworthy sources don't hold up under close scrutiny.

"Ridiculous!" you say, "Why would our own government (or the *New York Times*) want to lie about this?" Let's look.

Cherry-picked findings

The Centers for Disease Control and Prevention issued a warning rivaling a surgeon general's: "Mothers who smoke 10 or more cigarettes a day actually can cause as many as 26,000 new cases of asthma among their children each year." The origins of this phantom statistic are tucked away in back sections of the Environmental Protection Agency's unreadable tome on ETS—a near guarantee that no one actually will get to it. From my reading of it, however, I detected a postmodern evolution of Darwinian selectivity. The EPA carefully picked a subset of 10 existing studies on childhood asthma and ETS to review. Then, it fished within these studies to find the shark bait.

They decided to highlight only four of the 10 to base their assessment of increased risk of childhood asthma from ETS. Then the agency completely dismissed the one study showing absolutely no effect. Next, from the numerous results contained in the remaining three studies, the EPA considered only those they liked. After cherry-picking findings from the cherry-picked subset of their cherry-picked set of studies, the EPA number crunchers pronounced it "reasonable" to use a range of 75 percent to 125 percent as their estimated increased risk for developing asthma in children whose mothers smoke 10 or more cigarettes per day. They then creatively projected this increased risk to the entire population.

Highly publicized claims [on the dangers of secondhand smoke] from seemingly trustworthy sources don't hold up under close scrutiny.

Suddenly, between 8,000 to 26,000 new cases of childhood asthma could be attributable to mothers smoking 10 or more cigarettes a day, or so reads the government's report. And with another pass of the federal government's magic wand, another 26,000 new cases of childhood asthma could be seen as caused by moms who smoke half a pack.

Moving as if ETS were even more deadly than sarin gas, the Occupational Safety and Health Administration, or OSHA, in April 1994 proposed new regulations tantamount to a total ban on workplace smoking in the United States. For employers willing to foot the bill, the proposed rule would permit smoking areas only if "enclosed and exhausted directly to the outside, and maintained under negative pressure sufficient to contain the tobacco smoke." Additionally, no work of any kind is allowed in this smoking area. The only people permitted to enter this area to do any work would be cleaning staff.

How did OSHA come up with a rationale for this sweeping prohibition? First, they looked at all the 13 studies with findings on occupational ETS and lung-cancer risk. From these, OSHA chose only one on which to base its estimate of increased risk from workplace ETS. OSHA's reasoning: This particular study was large and well-designed. But so were others in this group! This was the only study among the 13 with a result to OSHA's liking.

Prohibitionist efforts

Opposed by a range of individuals and groups, OSHA's proposed rule generated more than 100,000 letters; the required public hearing lasted an unprecedented six months. The prohibition plan still seems alive and stubbornly kicking within the halls of Palace OSHA.

In an amazing feat of federal legerdemain, the Department of Transportation, or DOT, managed to convince the International Civil Aviation Organization (a U.N. agency) to pass a resolution that airliners should absolutely and universally prohibit smoking. DOT created its very own fat research report to reinforce its point.

This ban was scheduled for July 1996, but there's been a lot of foot-dragging. Do the foot-draggers know something others don't? Perhaps they actually read DOT's research report about ETS in airliner cabins, and after they stopped laughing, they tossed it.

The technique used by DOT was to measure the amount of "bad stuff" from tobacco smoke in the cabins' air. They expected to find higher concentrations in planes with smoking sections than in those without. Since smoking bans already were enforced on domestic flights, no-smoking planes readily were available for comparison. Their state-of-the-art measurements were surprising: Once past the "boundary rows" (the first three next to the smoking section), average levels of respirable particles and carbon dioxide actually were lower on smoking flights than on no-smoking flights. Average levels of nicotine were low enough to be undetectable past the boundary rows on the majority of flights. On the minority with detectable nicotine levels, the difference, measured in micrograms (1 billionth of 2.2 pounds) per cubic meter ($3\frac{1}{3}$ feet) of air was a minuscule $\frac{1}{20}$ of 1 microgram. Average carbon-monoxide levels were a rousing 0.2 micrograms per cubic meter higher on smoking flights! There were, however, 200 fewer parts per million of headache-making carbon dioxide on the smoking flights than on the nonsmoking.

But DOT had a mission. So their crystal ball predicted, over a span of 20 years, four excess lung cancer deaths among the entire U.S. cabin-crew population. Shazam! Then DOT declared that smoking should be extinguished from the skies, since it would be too expensive sufficiently to improve the ventilation and filtration of airline-cabin air. The expense? Twenty dollars per flight, max, or a big 36 cents per smoker on a full Boeing 747, or 93 cents on a 727. Incidentally, smoking isn't the only reason to improve airline ventilation.

Misleading statistics

Publicity about a recent study on ETS and acute or chronic respiratory illnesses in children admonishes, "Children exposed to tobacco smoke . . . suffer over 10 million days of restricted activities . . . 21 percent more than unexposed kids." Ten million is a catchy, scary number, but where does it come from? The study appeared in the May 13–18, 1996, issue of the "scientific" journal, *Tobacco Control*, the very title of which should raise questions about scientific objectivity. The authors show right up front that they failed to find a "statistically significant" relationship between the children's exposure to tobacco smoke and any respiratory illnesses.

But then they reported that the parents in their sample were asked how many days the children missed school or had their activities restricted. Somehow, the researchers "found" here the relationship they wanted—albeit small. No attempt was made to determine if other factors could account for this, nor was there any attempt to account for the contradiction.

The authors took their preferred finding, extrapolated it to the whole U.S. population and, eureka!, 10 million. Note: This number signifies only that, for unknown reasons, parents who smoked recalled keeping their kids home slightly more than parents who didn't, but it doesn't mean that the smokers' offspring were sicker. The researchers did not publicize the fact that the number of childhood illnesses linked to ETS exposure was negligible. This is misleading reporting.

Researchers did not publicize the fact that the number of childhood illnesses linked to ETS exposure was negligible. This is misleading reporting.

If the prohibitionists could make a convincing case that ETS causes heart disease (the leading killer in the United States) in nonsmokers, they'd be in clover. Even with a small excess risk from ETS, really big death estimates could balloon. The lack of hard evidence doesn't stop tobacco prohibitionists and their scientific allies from trying. Witness a front-page story in the *New York Times* on May 20, 1997: A team of Harvard researchers released the results of a 10-year study which claimed that regular exposure to other people's smoke at home or at work almost doubled the risk of heart disease. Case closed? Not according to Steve Milloy, executive director of The Advancement of Sound Science Coalition, who called the study another case of "epidemiologists trying to pass off junk science as Nobel prize work."

A day after the Harvard report was issued Milloy issued the following statement: "The new study uses statistics—not science—to claim that secondhand smoke increases the risk of heart attack by 91 percent. This abuse of statistics is such a problem that the National Cancer Institute issued a press release in 1994 advising that increases in risk of less than 100 percent were not to be trusted. And for good reason. In the new study, there was no measurement of even one person's exposure to secondhand smoke. The researchers relied on unverified questionnaires. Also, it is likely the researchers did not adequately consider other competing causes for heart disease such as smoking, lack of exercise, poor diet and so forth."

Divide, scare, and hector

Is there a pattern here? An Aug. 15, 1996, Associated Press bulletin claimed that the results of a huge study showed that never-smokers married to smokers had about a 20 percent higher risk of dying from heart disease than with nonsmoking mates. Actually, this result only applied to the never-smoking men married to current smokers. No excess risk was found for never-smoking women married to current smokers. Oops! They forgot to mention that part of it. And wouldn't there be more heart disease in the husbands of heavy smokers than of light smokers if, in fact, ETS exposure had something to do with it? But in this study, the finding was upside-down; the more the wife smoked, the lower the husband's risk. Hmmm! This piece of information also failed to appear in the AP story.

Since the 1960s, our government, aided by an assortment of do-gooders, has been trying to get everyone to quit smoking. It started out reasonably by disseminating information that smoking was linked to some nasty diseases. Having our best interests at heart, concerned professionals and government officials apparently felt compelled to devise stronger arguments to make us do the right thing. The government funded research in order to confirm the idea that ETS is harmful. But, the research results came in mostly indeterminate and, in some cases, negative. What to do? Well, since it's for a good cause, ignore the reality. Claim lots of dire findings. Divide, scare and hector.

8

The Tobacco Industry Markets Its Product to Youths

David Tannenbaum

David Tannenbaum is an intern at Multinational Monitor, *a monthly journal that focuses on the issues of labor, globalization, and corporate corruption.*

As a result of various lawsuits, several cigarette companies were required to release records documenting their intentional marketing of tobacco products to minors. These documents reveal that tobacco companies tracked their brands' popularity among teens, designed cigarette labels specifically for youths, and planned advertising campaigns to increase their market share among minors. In an attempt to deny allegations that they were targeting youths, the tobacco industry designed public relations programs and educational publications that emphasized the need for adults to help youths make responsible decisions about smoking. The intent of these programs was not to reduce teen smoking but to boost the public image of cigarette companies and to create the perception that the tobacco industry was addressing the problem of underage smoking.

For years, tobacco companies have claimed that they neither market to teenagers nor depend on them for decades of future profits. The tobacco documents used in the Minnesota State Attorney General's lawsuit against the companies and other documents that were released as a result of that suit disprove both of those claims.

Cigarette companies have long known which brands attract teenagers and the importance of capturing them as customers. In a 1987 Philip Morris (PM) interoffice memo discussing tactics to soften the blow of an upcoming excise tax increase, an executive writes, "You may recall from the article I sent you that Jeffrey Harris of the Massachusetts Institute of Technology calculated, on the basis of the Lewin and Coate data, that the 1982–3 round of price increases caused two million adults to quit smok-

Reprinted from David Tannenbaum, "Smoking Guns I: Marketing to Kids," *Multinational Monitor*, July/August 1998, by permission of *Multinational Monitor*.

ing and prevented 600,000 teenagers from starting to smoke. Those teen-agers are now 18–21 years old, and since about 70 percent of 18–21 year-olds and 35 percent of older smokers smoke a PM brand, this means that 700,000 of those adult quitters *had been* PM smokers and 420,000 of the non-starters *would have been* PM smokers. Thus, if Harris is right, we were hit disproportionately hard. We don't need to have that happen again."

A 1979 Philip Morris memo notes "Marlboro dominates in the 17 and younger age category, capturing over 50% of this market."

Cigarettes designed for youths

Companies not only tracked their shares of the teenage market, they also sought to increase their cut of the pie, sometimes going so far as to design cigarette types targeted specifically at young teenagers. With regard to Marlboro's dominance, a Lorillard executive wrote in a 1978 memo: "The success of NEWPORT has been fantastic during the past few years. Our profile taken locally shows this brand being purchased by black people (all ages), young adults (usually college age), but the base of our business is the high school student. . . . NEWPORT in the 1970's is turning into the Marlboro of the 60's and 70's. It is the 'In' brand to smoke if you want to be one of the group. Our problem is the younger consumer that does not desire a menthol cigarette. If that person desires a non-menthol, but wants to be part of the 'In group', he goes to Marlboro. Could we end the success story for Marlboro by furnishing the young adult consumers with a total category of 'In' brands? . . . I think the time is right to develop a NEWPORT NATURAL (non-menthol) cigarette to attract the young adult consumer desiring a non-menthol product."

R.J. Reynolds (RJR) also attempted to encroach on Philip Morris' young clientele with its own Camel campaign. A 1975 memo recom-mends that the national expansion of "the successfully tested 'Meet the Turk' ad campaign and new Marlboro-type blend is another step to meet our marketing objective: To increase our young adult franchise. To ensure increased and longer-term growth for CAMEL FILTER the brand must in-crease its share penetration among the 14–24 age group which have a new set of more liberal values and which represent tomorrow's cigarette busi-ness." The memo suggests "patience, persistence, and consistency will be needed" as the brand shifts appeal from older to younger smokers.

Cigarette companies have long known which brands attract teenagers and the importance of capturing them as customers.

Brown & Williamson was also in on the adolescent hunt, as a 1973 memo recognizes that *"KOOL has shown little or no growth in share of users in the 26+ age group. Growth is from 16–25 year olds. At the present rate, a smoker in the 16–25 year age group will soon be three times as important to KOOL as prospect in any other broad age category. . . . KOOL's stake in the 16–25 year old population segment is such that the value of this au-dience should be accurately weighted and reflected in current media programs. As a result, all magazines will be reviewed to see how efficiently they reach this group and other groups as well."

As time went on, the tobacco industry began to realize that its image as a peddler of tobacco products to children was beginning to hurt the bottom line. As calls for restrictions on print advertisements, sampling and sports sponsorship became more frequent, the industry cooked up various public relations schemes to rebut compelling charges that it was marketing to kids.

"Responsible living"

One of the industry's first major initiatives was the "Responsible Living Program," launched in September 1984. Through the Tobacco Institute, the companies published a booklet for parents and their teenagers entitled "Helping Youth Decide." The Tobacco Institute produced the publication in cooperation with the National Association of State Boards of Education (NASBE). It explained ways of speaking freely with teenagers about making "adult decisions," but contained no smoking-specific content.

To the public, the industry tried to portray its efforts as purely altruistic, with concern for children and parents at the fore. Reporting on responses to the Responsible Living Program, the Tobacco Institute claimed, "The anti-smokers were speechless. People genuinely interested in youth welfare were generous with praise and offers to help." Educators, civic leaders, Congressional members, the news media were all positive. Within two and a half months, more than 50,000 of the booklets had been "circulated to parents around the country." A presentation was made before the National Black Caucus of State Legislators and the Institute won a resolution endorsing the measure and suggesting that legislators encourage their member school boards to utilize "this unique resource."

Internal documents suggest the industry had multiple motivations for the initiative. First, the industry gained credibility by collaborating with the NASBE. A June 1985 progress report noted, "We could only guess . . . that because of the [National Association of State Boards of Education] partnership . . . the program might be difficult for our adversaries to damn."

Second, as with its concurrent collaboration with fire service associations, the program was used to "butter up" potential allies as a first step to forming coalitions on a whole range of issues. The same progress report explains, "Meantime, consultants of ours have used the [booklet] with perhaps two dozen Hispanic groups . . . in California and the Midwest . . . as a way to get a foot in the door to talk about other issues."

Finally, and most importantly, the program was used as a direct lobbying tool in fights against various tobacco restrictions. Before the program was launched, the institute and NASBE planned to send a letter and preview kit to "key state officials." Lobbyists in Texas, Minnesota, Massachusetts and California successfully used the project to "help offset panels, to deal with sampling bills and to help fight excises earmarked for public education." In the face of "incipient proposals for smoking restrictions and a sampling ban," an industry representative "exhibited this current project" and the "Board asked for ten more copies of the booklet and tabled its proposals."

The fight continues

By 1989, the industry had become even more nervous about pending anti-tobacco legislation and started to lay out plans for a more elaborate public relations campaign to show the industry's commitment to reducing teenage smoking. A Tobacco Institute "Tobacco Advertising Restrictions Working Group Report" noted that the industry had to "'put its money where its mouth is.' In short, we recommend that the Institute undertake an enhanced program of activities on the youth smoking issue, including new tactics designed to create a more activist and credible image. The activities should be able to withstand scrutiny. . . . We believe it is unlikely that the Institute's current activities could withstand such scrutiny."

The same report listed several rhetorical concerns over this new initiative, the first of which was: "There is some risk that efforts to discourage youth smoking could decrease tobacco sales, both immediately and over the long term." The response was: "This is true. However, the group agreed that, in the absence of credible industry efforts to address the youth smoking issue, various types of potential legislative and regulatory action likely would have a much more serious impact upon tobacco sales."

Another concern of the group was that "the youth smoking issue is not a substantial problem for the industry. No legislative battles have been lost on this issue to date." The response: "We believe this attitude to be short-sighted. The strategy on youth smoking has not so much become 'broke,' as simply inadequate for the job. . . . Our allies and potential allies need credible arguments to defend the industry on the issue; action is called for if the industry is to *maintain* its record of legislative success." The youth smoking issue tarnished the industry's image and was being used "to restrict tobacco advertising and promotion, . . . support excise tax legislation, and generally as a weapon to attack the industry's image and credibility." Somehow the industry needed "to discourage unnecessary and unfair restrictions that, directly or indirectly, adversely affect the legitimate and truthful brand advertising, promotional and marketing practices of the cigarette industry."

The [tobacco] industry cooked up various public relations schemes to rebut compelling charges that it was marketing to kids.

Thus, the working group developed "Strategy III," intended to "demonstrate that the industry does not want children to use its products and has taken positive steps to discourage such use."

Specific goals were to "Provide ammunition for tobacco allies (legislators and others). . . . Enhance the industry's overall ability to gain and maintain allies. . . . Help build the industry's image by demonstrating a sense of responsibility and corporate citizenship. . . . Enhance credibility by formulating strong programs and implementing them aggressively."

Direct tactics included a stronger voluntary youth practices code, support for introduction and enforcement of minimum smoking age laws, a retailer awareness program "to develop retailers as coalition partners in avoiding severe restrictions that could adversely impact their businesses (to a much greater degree than would the immediate loss in sales to minors)," more educational materials, coalition partners "from groups such as teachers' unions, guidance counselor organizations and the PTA, to convenience store chains and local chambers of commerce," media relations supported by coalition allies, research into smoking rates, and the causes of youth smoking.

Throughout the program, the Institute was concerned about the public's perception of its new programs. A strategy paper documents plans to commission focus groups to "'market test' the opinions and sentiments of opinion leaders and teachers, etc.," since "there needs to be either real ways to solve the problem or at least the perception that the problem is being addressed."

9

Tobacco Advertising Encourages People to Smoke

William Everett Bailey

William Everett Bailey is a longtime tobacco control advocate and the author of The Invisible Drug, *from which this viewpoint is excerpted.*

Cigarette advertising encourages people to smoke. Tobacco companies use images in their advertising that connote sophistication, independence, attractiveness, and rebelliousness, and these images persuade people to buy cigarettes. Moreover, cigarettes are prominently featured in movies, and tobacco company sponsorship ensures that cigarette brand names and poster ads pervade sporting events such as tennis tournaments and auto racing. To counter antismoking advocates' attempts to ban or restrict cigarette advertising, tobacco companies downplay the deadly effects of tobacco use and emphasize smoking as a legal individual choice and right. Tobacco promotional efforts have been so effective that even nonsmokers often view smoking as innocuous and socially acceptable.

Advertising affects everyone. We just do not like to admit it.
—Professor Edward Popper, North Eastern University

What made cigarettes the most successful product in American history? Advertising. No one likes to admit that advertising has an effect on them. Most people will agree that they do not like to be "sold." Despite this, advertising works. It makes people buy brand name products, and products on sale.

Cigarette advertising reached an unprecedented high of $3.27 billion in 1988. Since then, the budget steadily increased, and by 1993 was $6.2 billion. That is $24 spent for every person in the U.S., or about $135 per smoker. This is the largest ad campaign in the history of any product.

The tobacco industry must replace the smokers that die or quit. Tobacco companies claim they use tobacco advertising to attract two classes of buyers. Brand competition advertising is designed to switch existing smokers away from another brand. The other class of buyer is the new smoker or starter. The easiest and most vulnerable new smoker is the teenager.

Reprinted from Chapter 4 of William Everett Bailey, *The Invisible Drug* (Houston: Mosaic Publications, 1996), by permission of the publisher.

Guy Smith, a Philip Morris public relations executive, explains "Our studies, and anti-smokers research say the top three reasons people start smoking are: 1) Advertising, 2) Friends smoke, and 3) Family members smoke."

Creating a desire to smoke

> I never saw an ad that made someone buy something they did not want.
>
> —John O' Toole, President,
> American Association of Advertising Agencies

This is true for selling cigarettes. Salespeople will tell you that you have to desire something before you want to buy it. Desire precedes want. Cigarette ads create a desire. Teens desire popularity, acceptance, something in common with a peer group, and to rebel against adults. Women desire equality to men, a sense of importance, and recognition.

• *Targeting women.* Until the 1920's, tobacco advertising mainly targeted males. Men were smoking, but the industry was missing the female segment of the market. American Tobacco Company's Lucky Strike campaign in 1927 finally broke the social barrier that frowned on women smoking. This campaign started women smoking by creating desire—the desire for women to be equal to men. Smoking was portrayed as the thing to do to give women the equality they desired. When women desired equality, they wanted to smoke.

The advertising genius, Dr. Edward Bernays, was credited for breaking the barrier. (Later, Bernays worked aggressively for pro-health, tobacco control organizations.) Bernays consulted a psychoanalyst, Dr. A.A. Brill, about the challenge. Dr. Brill explained, "Cigarettes, to women, are torches of freedom that they use to dramatize their objection of the taboo against smoking by men."

At the next Easter Parade, debutantes were solicited to march and smoke, that is to light "torches of freedom," in protest to man's inhumanity to women. Within six weeks of the promotion, the barrier was broken. Smoking by women became accepted, and Lucky Strikes became the best seller. Slogans such as "Reach for a Lucky instead of a sweet" were used. Famous people, like Lucille Ball, Dean Martin, Bob Hope, Henry Fonda, Arthur Godfrey, and Jerry Lewis appeared in advertisements.

What made cigarettes the most successful product in American history? Advertising.

One Lucky Strike ad read: "An ancient prejudice has been removed. Today, legally, politically and socially, womanhood stands in her true light. American intelligence has cast aside the ancient prejudice that held her to be inferior."

The dramatic rise in women smoking can be attributed to that one Lucky Strike advertising and promotion campaign. Advertising did not cause women to switch from one brand to another. Advertising directly induced women to start smoking, a fact the tobacco industry denies.

Janet Sackman began smoking when she appeared as "Miss Lucky Strike" in advertisements. "They kept providing false reassurances," that she says encouraged her to start smoking, "so I had no idea that smoking was so very dangerous." Some years later Ms. Sackman developed throat cancer, and is a tobacco control advocate today.

• *Tobacco advertising in women's magazines.* In the late 1960's and 1970's, major advertising campaigns were initiated for Virginia Slims, Silva Thins and Eve cigarettes. Advertising that targets women uses themes of liberation and feminism, and images of sophistication and slimness. Virginia Slims was introduced in 1968 using the theme "You've come a long way, baby."

Today, women's magazines that run cigarette advertisements have fewer articles on the health hazards of smoking. Some of the most widely circulated magazines today collect more than 25% of their advertising income from tobacco advertising. The editors will not run articles on the hazards of smoking because they do not want to lose the tobacco company's advertising money.

• *Doctors were used to promote cigarette safety.* In the 1950's, doctors were solicited to promote the safety of smoking. These ads reassured the public about the safety of cigarettes: "More doctors smoke Camels than any other cigarette." "20,679 physicians preferred to smoke a Lucky Strike because it's toasted."

[Cigarette] advertising that targets women uses themes of liberation and feminism, and images of sophistication and slimness.

Philip Morris advertisements targeted physicians. Real doctors appeared in their cigarette advertisements. They appealed to other doctors to recommend Philip Morris to their patients. One such ad appearing in a medical journal stated: "With proof so conclusive . . . (that Philip Morris are less irritating) . . . with your own personal experience added to the published studies. Would it not be good practice to suggest Philip Morris to your patients who smoke?"

• *The Marlboro Man.* Philip Morris began the Marlboro country theme in television advertisements in 1964. The Western theme painted portraits of ruggedness and independence, with cattle, boots, cowboy hats, all sprinkled with testosterone overtones. The center piece of the theme was the famous "Marlboro Man."

R.W. Murry, Philip Morris CEO, stated that the Marlboro Man conveys "elements of adventure, freedom, being in charge of your own destiny." Marlboros give the adolescent a badge to identify them as masculine, in the same way a car, clothes or a cologne do. Some kids see the Marlboro Man as an outlaw, and smoking Marlboro gives them a way to be "bad."

The Marlboro cowboy is said to be one of the most successful advertising icons ever. The actor that immortalized the Marlboro Man on TV ads was David McLean, who died of lung cancer on October 12, 1995, at the age of 73. Following the advertising ban on TV, a new Marlboro Man portrayed the famous cowboy on billboards and printed ads. His name was Wayne McLaren. McLaren died of lung cancer on July 23, 1992, at the age of 51. Some of his last words were: "Take care of the children. Tobacco will kill you, and I am living proof of it."

The Marlboro country advertising campaign has made Marlboro the number one selling cigarette. That campaign is still promoted in the 1990's. Today, one third of the 46 million smokers in America smoke Marlboro. In 1995, the brand was honored by the American Marketing Association by naming Marlboro to their hall of fame.

The Marlboro Man is not the only cigarette model that has fallen victim to lung cancer. Alan Landers was a Winston billboard and magazine model in the 1960's. He has since undergone two operations for lung cancer. Mr. Landers is now a spokesman for a pro-health, tobacco control group, Citizens for A Tobacco-free Society.

Smoking in the movies

Movies in the 50's romanticized smoking. Some of the early Hollywood image makers were Marlon Brando, Humphrey Bogart, and Bette Davis. Smoking became a positive statement of American culture. Most baby boomers, statistically about half, were raised by parents that smoked.

A study of films, from 1960 to 1990, revealed:

- Smoking in films was three times as prevalent as it was in the general population.
- Smokers were portrayed as successful, attractive, white males.
- Smoking was associated with hostility and stress reduction.
- The incidence of young people smoking in films doubled during that time.

The exaggerated prevalence of smoking in films misleads young people to overestimate the real prevalence of cigarette smoking. "Everybody smokes," is an answer often given by adolescents as a reason for smoking.

The high rate of smoking in films is the result of tobacco companies paying producers to 'place' their brand of cigarettes in movies, a common practice before 1990. Tobacco companies often gave payments of cash, cars, jewelry, and even horses to the cast and crew. In the 1980's, Philip Morris paid $350,000 to have their cigarettes in the James Bond movie, *License to Kill*. Brown & Williamson Tobacco Corp. (B.A.T.) paid almost $700,000 to producers to have Kool in movies, such as *Body Heat*.

Sylvester Stallone was allegedly paid $300,000 to show a Kool billboard for a few seconds in *First Blood*. Stallone recently denied ever receiving any money from B.A.T., and says he does not enter into such agreements today.

No movie was immune to paid cigarette promotions— they also appeared in children's movies. *Who Framed Roger Rabbit*, and *Honey I Shrunk the Kids*, both Walt Disney movies, had Camel "ads" in them.

Tobacco companies, in response to public outrage in 1990, agreed to stop the practice of paying to have their brands in movies. However, many producers independently continue to glamorize smoking by having leading stars and role models for America's youth smoke. One 1994 example is Winona Ryder's part as a nicotine addicted youth in the movie *Reality Bites*. Hollywood idols, such as Johnny Depp and Brad Pitt, have also depicted smoking as the trendy, cool thing to do.

Banned from television?

Cigarette manufacturers spent about $300 million on television advertising in 1967. Before 1967, the American TV watching public was exposed to few pro-health, tobacco control messages. Then in July of 1967, the Fairness Doctrine required equal time for antismoking messages, largely due to the work of the pro-health tobacco control advocacy organization Action on Smoking and Health (ASH). About $75 million in air time was provided for smoking cessation and prevention messages. For the first time, TV watchers saw both tobacco advertising and antismoking messages. That mix continued until January 1971, when all advertising on TV and radio was banned. This also put an end to the smoking cessation and prevention messages. It is most important to note that during the era when health messages encouraged people to quit smoking, cigarette consumption dropped seven percent. Furthermore, once the pro-health messages were eliminated, cigarette consumption jumped back up. This is a mammoth study that provides evidence that advertising works, and that smoking cessation and prevention messages are effective in countering cigarette advertising.

The year following the advertising ban in 1971, the decision was tested by the U.S. Supreme Court and upheld as constitutional. Despite the ban, cigarette advertisements still can be seen today on most televised sports events.

Tobacco advertising at sporting events

Tobacco company sponsorship of sporting events totaled $84 million in 1988. Cigarette billboard ads are prominently displayed at televised sports events like tennis tournaments, baseball, and auto racing. Hanging from the wall surrounding the action, they often appear on TV. One report claims Philip Morris was guaranteed three minutes of TV exposure of its cigarette advertisement during a Knicks game at Madison Square Garden.

• *Baseball.* Philip Morris is baseball's third largest sign advertiser. One of the most famous signs is their Marlboro Man ad at New York's Shea Stadium. On May 21, 1995, ASH filed a complaint with the Department of Justice about these signs. The Justice Department charged that Philip Morris placed ads in strategic locations to appear on TV. Philip Morris has used this loophole in the ban on TV cigarette advertising for 24 years. They finally complied with the Justice Department's demand to stop the practice, but only after a six month battle.

The Justice Department's agreement with Philip Morris does not include auto racing. Meanwhile, the cigarette logo race cars continue to jump through the loophole in the ban on TV advertising—a loophole the Food and Drug Administration (FDA) wants to close.

• *Tobacco advertising at auto racing events.* Auto racing is the biggest arena for tobacco advertising. Philip Morris and R.J. Reynolds (RJR) spend about $30 million a year on auto racing cigarette promotions, filling about

12 hours of air time a week. Sponsorship of the Nascar's Winston Cup gets RJR about 30 hours of TV coverage for Winston. RJR has spent $200 million on Nascar racing since 1971. During a televised Marlboro Grand Prix race tobacco advertising flashed across the screen constantly. Dr. Alan Blum M.D., of Doctors Ought to Care (DOC), had the patience to count the number of times the Marlboro logo appeared—5,933 times.

Other promotional efforts

• *Free cigarette samples.* Doling out free drugs is one of the most effective ways to induce drug dependence in a vulnerable person. Free cigarette giveaways at community and sporting events is part of tobacco companies' promotional strategy. In 1993, cigarette companies spent $2.6 billion on free samples, coupons and other financial incentives to hook smokers.

At one time, airline food trays were served with a pack containing three cigarettes, even to kids. Today, auto racing is a typical event where cigarettes are given away. Tobacco salesmen have also been known to toss bushel baskets of cigarettes at passersby in the streets of New York City. One witness to this described the cigarette giveaway as causing a near riot.

In 1992, The State of New York passed the *No Tobacco Sampling Law.* Later in 1994, Philip Morris mailed five packages of Marlboro to 44,000 people in New York. If a young person intercepted and smoked all five packs they would have a 94% chance of becoming nicotine dependent, and one of every three would die from tobacco related diseases. Philip Morris paid $250,000 to the state in a settlement, while denying their guilt.

In 1995, Philip Morris announced that it was indefinitely suspending all cigarette sampling. In contrast, an RJR spokesperson said we "feel very comfortable" with our current sampling programs, and have "no plans to suspend them."

• *Funding of Community and Special Events.* Event sponsorship increases brand visibility, and associates a particular lifestyle with a brand to create loyalty. In 1994, event sponsorship rose to more than $4 billion.

Concerts are one kind of community activity tobacco companies commonly fund. Youth-oriented concerts are frequently targeted for free cigarette sample giveaways. Tobacco companies also fund minority organizations, such as the United Negro College Fund, which receives $150,000 a year. Some museums also rely on tobacco donations.

Smoking cessation and prevention messages are effective in countering cigarette advertising.

To the tobacco zealots, utopia is selling cigarettes the way they did in the 1950's. At that time, nearly half the country smoked, and the tobacco industry operated with even fewer government regulations. They advertised their tobacco products without restrictions, and denied all the health hazards of smoking.

Past advertising themes were associated with high-style living, healthy activities, economic, social, and professional success. Today, cigarette advertising campaigns are tailored to children, women, blue-collar workers, and minorities. The young and hip are being wooed by RJR and Philip Morris with trendy packaging and artsy imaging, with brands such as Red Kamel and Moonlight.

Whatever the message, whatever the product, they are all the same old cancer sticks. Ads avoid the health hazards of smoking. They deny the health hazards attributed to environmental tobacco smoke (ETS) and deny that nicotine is addictive. They divert our attention from these issues with institutional advertising that concentrates on rights, freedom, choice and government interference.

With help of the American Civil Liberties Union, the tobacco industry has tried to link the ban on advertising with the issue of free speech. They claim First Amendment rights. The ban on TV advertising has been tested, and failed to qualify as a violation of the First Amendment. It is important to note that the Supreme Court ruled that advertising was a "low form of speech," and was not considered at all protected by the First Amendment. Scholars agree that if Congress or the FDA ban all tobacco advertising, the Supreme Court would uphold the ban as constitutional.

Sidestepping the issue

A study sponsored by the Tobacco Institute in 1978 warned that the most dangerous development to the tobacco business is the public's concern about ETS. The Roper Organization did a public poll on smoking, and made these recommendations:

- The tobacco industry's strategy should be a program of publicity to show ETS is not harmful.
- They should argue that a vote for a new tobacco excise tax is a vote against freedom and rights.
- To take the position that a vote for a Smoke-free Environment Act is a vote for more arrests, and overworked police officers chasing smokers.
- To sidestep the health issue, and draw fire from it by talking about rights, privacy, government intervention, big brother, freedom and civil liberties. (Variation used today: accommodation).

Roper created the "What's Next Defense," a series of sidestepping tactics for the tobacco industry. Their overall strategy attempts to undermine reasonable tobacco control efforts by confusing the issue with exaggerated and sometimes ridiculous claims. The "What's Next Defense" applied to a ban on tobacco advertising would sound like this: "What's next—a ban on coffee advertising?"

The tobacco industry was quick to put Roper's advice into practice to ward off all tobacco control efforts, and is still using it today. Seventeen years after the Roper Report, Guy L. Smith, VP of Philip Morris in 1987, used the "What's Next Defense" when he said: "If those that oppose tobacco would succeed in dictating which behaviors were acceptable and which were not, . . . If they eliminated free choice regarding tobacco, they would affect free choice itself. What would they ban next? Alcohol, red meat, eggs, dairy products?"

Smith compares taking a poison to eating food. These stale "What's next messages" still appear in editorials, and in tobacco industry propaganda today:

- Will alcohol be next?
- Will caffeine be next?
- Will high fat foods be next?
- Ban books, movies, music?
- Where will it all end?
- A cigarette ban is the beginning of the end of a free country!

The common thread running through all this sidestepping is to divert the public's attention from the real issues—tobacco use and secondhand smoke kills people!

Beware of the opinions of those tobacco zealots who support smoking in public, deny the health hazards of secondhand smoke, or deny that nicotine is addictive. Former senator and presidential candidate Bob Dole, for example, in July 1996 stated in public that he did not think nicotine was addictive.

Some editorials are written by tobacco industry consultants who are paid to promote their position. Use caution if the source of information quoted is from the Tobacco Institute. If so it is probably biased, misleading, or incorrect. Observe some of their sidestepping strategy regarding banning smoking in public:

It's an attack on individual rights. An attack on freedom of choice. Not allowing smoking in public is government intervention, prohibition, discrimination. (Roper: Sidestep the health issue by talking about rights, privacy, government intervention, big brother, freedom and civil liberties.)

ETS is not the same as mainstream smoke. (Roper: The tobacco industry's strategy should be a program of publicity to show ETS is not harmful. This is also a half-truth. ETS has more carcinogens than mainstream smoke, and it kills people.)

Smokers will become criminals overnight. (Roper: Take the position that a vote for banning smoking in public is a vote for more arrests, and overworked police officers chasing smokers. Experience from cities where smoking is banned in public shows that no arrests have been necessary because smokers willingly comply with the ban.)

The young and hip are being wooed by RJR and Philip Morris with trendy packaging and artsy imaging, with brands such as Red Kamel and Moonlight.

Not every newspaper reader in every major city is fortunate enough to have newspapers with editorial boards that are pro-health. Consider that many editorial boards are like most folks—they are deficient in their knowledge of the hazards of smoking, secondhand smoke, and nicotine addiction. Furthermore, they have been neutralized by tobacco advertising in two ways. First, tobacco advertising makes them complacent, and they suffer from the "friendly familiarity" syndrome. Second, they have become accustomed to the significant profits made from tobacco advertisements.

On the other hand, some reporters have done a tremendous job in unraveling many of the tobacco companies' deceptions. Alix Freedman, a reporter for the *Wall Street Journal*, won the Pulitzer Prize in 1996 for uncovering deception in the tobacco industry. For that, the tobacco industry has lashed out at reporters, claiming that:

- Reporters do not trust the tobacco industry, and are one sided on the issue.
- The press is not fair because they allow more space for scientists and doctors to argue the health hazards of ETS than the tobacco industries' position.
- One should trust the tobacco industry, not journalists, for reliable health information on ETS.

"Risky activity"

The tobacco industry, using expert psychologists as advertising consultants, have found ways to confuse the health issue. One way to confuse the health issue is to call tobacco use a risky activity. They compare smoking to sky diving, eating bacon, having unprotected sex, and drinking beer. Pointing a gun at your head and pulling the trigger can be called a risky activity. Smoking, like Russian Roulette, is also a deadly activity.

Bob Dole, in June 1996, compared the hazards of secondhand smoke to drinking milk. It is no coincidence that Philip Morris also has an active disinformation program running in Europe, which compares the hazards of secondhand smoke to eating cookies and milk. The message is that secondhand smoke is as harmless to a child as an all-American snack. Recall that in the ranking of preventable deaths, exposure to secondhand smoke was fifth. The truth is that food is essential to life—tobacco ends life.

Whenever a new tobacco excise tax is mentioned, it is called a risky activities tax. Similarly, as the heat is being turned up and several states are preparing to sue the tobacco companies for reimbursement for Medicaid expenses used to treat smokers' diseases, the tobacco companies are doing a double sidestep dance. They try to minimize the death and disease from tobacco use, and their responsibility for it, by saying that states are suing them because tobacco use is a risky activity. The tobacco companies defend smoking as if someone's life was at stake. Smoking is not essential to life—it is a cause of death. [In a 1998 civil settlement, the tobacco industry agreed to pay forty-six states $206 billion and submit to advertising and marketing restrictions.]

Whether it is a ban on advertising or smoking in public, the tobacco industry, and all the people that profit from tobacco use often defend their actions by whining "Tobacco is a legal product." Some other legal products are cocaine, morphine, amphetamine, barbiturate, and dynamite. At one time, LSD was a legal product. Most products that are not illegal have some kind of restrictions on their possession or use in the interest of public health and safety. Why should tobacco be any different from other legal products that are restricted to protect the health of the public?

The legal product defense used in this context is saying "you can not restrict the use of a legal product," which is a half-truth. On the other hand, when the legal product defense is used by a tobacco company attorney it may have a different meaning. When asked about the deaths of ten million smokers, they answer with the same legal product defense but with this meaning: "Yes, but tobacco is a legal product and there's nothing you can do about it."

Who knows where the tobacco industry got their moral values? One ad actually touted smoking as morally right. If that is so, then it must follow that it is morally right to poison yourself, abuse addictive drugs, and kill other people by poisoning. Furthermore, what they do must be morally right as well: the manufacture, distribution, promotion and advertising of an addictive drug that has killed ten million people. And selling addictive poisons to children must be morally right. This moral code also implies that if a generous profit is made, it is morally right.

Some people want to stop tobacco advertising because it conflicts with their moral beliefs. One concerned group is the Interfaith Center of Corporate Responsibility, a coalition of Roman Catholic, Protestant, and Jewish institutional investors. Some 275 coalition members advocate corporate responsibility on issues such as tobacco advertising.

Outdoor billboard advertising is one way tobacco advertising reaches children. According to the Outdoor Advertising Association of America (OAAA), the three largest billboard companies are Gannett Outdoor, Eller Media Co., and 3M Media. In May of 1996, the Interfaith Center of Corporate Responsibility led the way to convince 3M that they should stop accepting billboard advertising from tobacco companies.

When Kippy Burns, a spokesperson for OAAA, was asked about 3M's action on tobacco advertising she said that they will continue a "firm and vigilant support of free-speech protections." Once again, the Roper Report strategy was used to avoid the health issue by invoking the first amendment.

Unfortunately, the first and second largest billboard advertisers, Gannett Outdoor and Eller Media Co., are not going to follow 3M's moral decision. Jeffrey Dixon, spokesperson for Eller Media said "As long as tobacco continues to be legal, we will continue to advertise it"—using the legal product defense. Philip Morris' response was a predictable "cigarette ads help adults make choices."

The perception of smoking is conditioned by advertising—by associating smoking with psychological traits. An advertising executive for Philip Morris called this "friendly familiarity." Many nonsmokers also view smoking as socially acceptable. Too many have been lulled into a state of numbness—often sitting in smoking sections with no concern. On the contrary, others are less tolerant in their acceptance of smoking in public. If all 214 million nonsmokers were more aware of the seriousness of the health hazards of secondhand smoke, more would take action to stop smoking in public places; 83,000 lives a year depend on it.

10

Tobacco Advertising Should Not Be Banned

Jacob Sullum

Jacob Sullum is a senior editor of Reason, *a monthly libertarian maga-zine. He is also the author of* For Your Own Good: The Anti-Smoking Crusade and the Tyranny of Public Health, *from which this view-point is adapted.*

Many researchers, antismoking activists, and public health advo-cates contend that tobacco advertising should be restricted or banned because it encourages people—particularly teenagers—to take up smoking. Yet there is no conclusive proof that people smoke because of exposure to cigarette ads and tobacco promo-tional items. Although ads may have an effect on an individual's cigarette brand preference, advertising does not necessarily con-vince people to start smoking. Banning tobacco advertising in an effort to reduce teen smoking would be nothing more than cen-sorship. Curbing underage smoking is ultimately the responsibil-ity of concerned individuals, families, and law enforcement.

On January 1, 1971, the Marlboro Man rode across the television screen one last time. At midnight a congressional ban on broadcast advertis-ing of cigarettes went into effect, and the smoking cowboy was banished to the frozen land of billboards and print ads. With the deadline looming, bleary-eyed, hung-over viewers across the country woke to a final burst of cigarette celebration. "Philip Morris went on a $1.25-million ad binge New Year's Day on the Dick Cavett, Johnny Carson and Merv Griffin shows," the *New York Times* reported. "There was a surfeit of cigarette ads during the screening of the bowl games." And then they were gone. American TV viewers would no longer be confronted by happy smokers frolicking on the beach or by hapless smokers losing the tips of their extralong cigarettes between cymbals and elevator doors. They would no longer have to choose between good grammar and good taste.

This was widely considered an important victory for consumers. The *Times* wondered whether the ad ban was "a signal that the voice of the consumer, battling back, can now really make itself heard in Washington." A *New Yorker* article tracing the chain of events that led to the ban concluded, "To an increasing degree, citizens of the consumer state seem to be perceiving their ability to turn upon their manipulators, to place widespread abuses of commercial privilege under the prohibition of laws that genuinely do protect the public, and, in effect, to give back to the people a sense of controlling their own lives."

Advertising as overpowering force

As these comments suggest, supporters of the ban viewed advertising not as a form of communication but as a mysterious force that seduces people into acting against their interests. This was a common view then and now, popularized by social critics such as Vance Packard and John Kenneth Galbraith. In *The Affluent Society* (1958), Galbraith argued that manufacturers produce goods and then apply "ruthless psychological pressures" through advertising to create demand for them. In *The Hidden Persuaders* (1957), Packard described advertising as an increasingly precise method of manipulation that can circumvent the conscious mind, influencing consumers without their awareness. He reinforced his portrait of Madison Avenue guile with the pseudoscientific concept of subliminal messages: seen but not seen, invisibly shaping attitudes and actions. The impact of such ideas can be seen in the controversy over tobacco advertising. The federal court that upheld the ban on broadcast ads for cigarettes quoted approvingly from another ruling that referred to "the subliminal impact of this pervasive propaganda."

There is remarkably little evidence that people smoke because of messages from tobacco companies.

Eliminating TV and radio commercials for cigarettes, of course, did not eliminate criticism of tobacco advertising. In 1985 the American Cancer Society, which decades earlier had called for an end to cigarette ads through "voluntary self-regulation," endorsed a government ban on all forms of tobacco advertising and promotion. The American Medical Association, the American Public Health Association, the American Heart Association, and the American Lung Association also began advocating a ban. Beginning in the mid-'80s, members of Congress introduced legislation that would have prohibited tobacco advertising, limited it to "tombstone" messages (black text on a white background), or reduced its tax deductibility. None of these bills got far.

In the '90s, since Congress did not seem inclined to impose further censorship on the tobacco companies, David Kessler, commissioner of the Food and Drug Administration (FDA), decided to do it by bureaucratic fiat. Reversing the FDA's longstanding position, he declared that the agency had jurisdiction over tobacco products. In August 1996 the FDA issued regulations aimed at imposing sweeping restrictions on the advertising and promotion of cigarettes and smokeless tobacco. Among other things, the regulations prohibited promotional items such as hats, T-shirts, and lighters; forbade brand-name sponsorship of sporting events; banned outdoor advertising within 1,000 feet of a playground, elementary school, or high school; and imposed a tombstone format on all other outdoor signs, all indoor signs in locations accessible to minors, and all print ads except those in publications with a negligible audience under the age of 18.

The tobacco companies challenged the regulations in federal court, and in April 1997 U.S. District Judge William L. Osteen ruled that the FDA had no statutory authority to regulate the advertising and promotion of "restricted devices," the category in which the agency had placed cigarettes and smokeless tobacco. Under the nationwide liability settlement proposed in June 1997, however, the tobacco companies agreed not only to the FDA rules but to additional restrictions, including bans on outdoor ads, on the use of human or cartoon figures, on Internet advertising, and on product placement in movies, TV shows, or video games. Congress is considering that proposal now, and any legislation that emerges will dramatically change the way tobacco companies promote their products. [After modification, this proposed settlement was finalized in November 1998.] Not content to wait, cities across the country, including New York, Chicago, and San Francisco, are imposing their own limits on cigarette signs and billboards. Elsewhere, the European Union plans to ban almost all forms of tobacco advertising by 2006.

These restrictions are based on the premise that fewer ads will mean fewer smokers—in particular, that teenagers will be less inclined to smoke if they are not exposed to so many images of rugged cowboys and pretty women with cigarettes. As a PTA official put it in 1967, "The constant seduction of cigarette advertising . . . gives children the idea that cigarettes are associated with all they hold dear—beauty, popularity, sex, athletic success." For three decades the debate over tobacco advertising has been driven by such concerns. Yet there is remarkably little evidence that people smoke because of messages from tobacco companies. The ready acceptance of this claim reflects a widespread view of advertising as a kind of magic that casts a spell on consumers and leads them astray.

Today's critics of capitalism continue to elaborate on the theme that Vance Packard and John Kenneth Galbraith got so much mileage out of in the '50s and '60s. Alan Thein Durning of the anti-growth Worldwatch Institute describes the "salient characteristics" of advertising this way: "It preys on the weaknesses of its host. It creates an insatiable hunger. And it leads to debilitating over-consumption. In the biological realm, things of that nature are called parasites." When combined with appeals to protect children, this perception of advertising as insidious and overpowering tends to squelch any lingering concerns about free speech.

Busting Joe Camel's hump

In 1988 R.J. Reynolds gave the anti-smoking movement an emblem for the corrupting influence of tobacco advertising. Introduced with the slogan "smooth character," Joe Camel was a cartoon version of the dromedary (known as Old Joe) that has appeared on packages of Camel cigarettes since 1913. Print ads and billboards depicted Joe Camel shooting pool in a tuxedo, hanging out at a nightclub, playing in a blues band, sitting on a motorcycle in a leather jacket and shades. He was portrayed as cool, hip, and popular—in short, he was like a lot of other models in a lot of other cigarette ads, except he was a cartoon animal instead of a flesh-and-blood human being. Even in that respect he was hardly revolutionary. More than a century before the debut of Joe Camel, historian Jordan Goodman notes, the manufacturer of Bull Durham smoking tobacco ran newspaper ads throughout the country depicting the Durham Bull "in anthropomorphic situations, alternating between scenes in which the bull was jovial and boisterous and those where he was serious and determined."

But Joe Camel, it is safe to say, generated more outrage than any other cartoon character in history. Critics of the ad campaign said the use of a cartoon was clearly designed to appeal to children. *Washington Post* columnist Courtland Milloy said "packaging a cartoon camel as a 'smooth character' is as dangerous as putting rat poison in a candy wrapper." In response to such criticism, R.J. Reynolds noted that Snoopy sold life insurance and the Pink Panther pitched fiberglass insulation, yet no one assumed those ads were aimed at kids.

[One] study . . . confirmed that . . . most 6-year-olds correctly associate [Joe Camel] with cigarettes. Yet 85 percent of the kids in this study had a negative attitude toward cigarettes.

The controversy intensified in 1991, when the *Journal of the American Medical Association* (*JAMA*) published three articles purporting to show that Joe Camel was indeed a menace to the youth of America. The heavily promoted studies generated an enormous amount of press coverage, under headlines such as "Camels for Kids" (*Time*), "I'd Toddle a Mile for a Camel" (*Newsweek*), "Joe Camel Is Also Pied Piper, Research Finds" (*Wall Street Journal*), and "Study: Camel Cartoon Sends Kids Smoke Signals" (*Boston Herald*). Dozens of editorialists and columnists condemned Joe Camel, and many said he should be banned from advertising.

In March 1992 the Coalition on Smoking or Health, a joint project of the American Cancer Society, the American Heart Association, and the American Lung Association, asked the Federal Trade Commission (FTC) to prohibit further use of the smooth character. Surgeon General Antonia Novello and the American Medical Association also called for an end to the campaign. In August 1993 the FTC's staff backed the coalition's petition, and a month later 27 state attorneys general added their support. In June 1994, by a 3-to-2 vote, the FTC decided not to proceed against Joe, finding that the record did not show he had increased smoking among minors. (During the first five years of the campaign, in fact, teenage smoking actually declined, starting to rise only in 1993.) In March 1997, after several members of Congress asked the FTC to re-examine the issue, the commission's staff again urged a ban, citing new evidence that R.J. Reynolds had targeted underage smokers. This time the commission, with two new members appointed by the Clinton administration, decided to seek an order instructing RJR not only to keep Joe out of children's sight but to conduct a "public education campaign" aimed at deterring underage smoking.

The two dissenting commissioners were not impressed by the new evidence, which failed to show that Joe Camel had actually encouraged kids to smoke. One wrote, "As was true three years ago, intuition and concern for children's health are not the equivalent of—and should not be substituted for—evidence sufficient to find reason to believe that there is a likely causal connection between the Joe Camel advertising campaign and smoking by children." But the FTC's action turned out to be doubly irrelevant. R.J. Reynolds, along with its competitors, agreed to stop using cartoon characters as part of the proposed nationwide settlement, and in July 1997 it announced that it was discontinuing the "smooth character" campaign, replacing it with one that makes more subtle use of camels.

Although the *JAMA* articles were widely cited by Joe's enemies, including the FTC and President Bill Clinton, they proved much less than the uproar would lead one to believe. In the first study, researchers led by Paul M. Fischer, a professor of family medicine at the Medical College of Georgia, asked preschoolers to match brand logos to pictures of products. Overall, about half the kids correctly matched Joe Camel with a cigarette. Among the 6-year-olds, the share was 91 percent, about the same as the percentage who correctly matched the Disney Channel logo to a picture of Mickey Mouse.

But recognizing Joe Camel is not tantamount to smoking, any more than recognizing the logos for Ford and Chevrolet (which most of the kids also did) is tantamount to driving. The researchers seemed to assume that familiarity breeds affection, but that is not necessarily the case. A subsequent study, funded by R.J. Reynolds and published in the Fall 1995 *Journal of Marketing*, confirmed that recognition of Joe Camel rises with age and that most 6-year-olds correctly associate him with cigarettes. Yet 85 percent of the kids in this study had a negative attitude toward cigarettes, and the dislike rose with both age and recognition ability. Among the 6-year-olds, less than 4 percent expressed a positive attitude toward cigarettes.

Animal magnetism

In the second *JAMA* study, Joseph R. DiFranza, a researcher at the University of Massachusetts Medical School, led a team that showed Joe Camel ads to samples of high school students and adults. They found that the teenagers were more likely to recognize Joe Camel, to recall the ads, and to evaluate them positively than the adults, whose average age was about 40. Since R.J. Reynolds contended that the Joe Camel campaign was aimed at young adults, these results were hardly surprising. Based on such comparisons, it is impossible to distinguish between an ad aimed at 16-year-olds and an ad aimed at 18-year-olds (or 21-year-olds).

DiFranza et al.'s most striking claim was that the Joe Camel campaign had caused a huge shift in brand preferences. Using data from seven surveys conducted in three states between 1976 and 1988, they estimated that 0.5 percent of underage smokers preferred Camels before the campaign began. By comparison, 33 percent of the teenage smokers in their study, conducted during 1990 and 1991, said they smoked Camels—a 66-fold increase. "Our data demonstrate that in just 3 years Camel's Old Joe cartoon character had an astounding influence on children's smoking behavior," the researchers wrote. But the pre-1989 surveys and the *JAMA* study were not comparable, and neither used random samples of the national population, so it's doubtful that the results are representative of American teenagers in general. Data from the Centers for Disease Control and Prevention's Teenage Attitudes and Practices Survey (TAPS), which does use a nationwide sample, suggest a much less dramatic (though still sizable) shift toward Camels. In 1993, 13.3 percent of the TAPS respondents said they usually bought Camels, compared to 8.1 percent in 1989.

Building brand loyalty among teenagers is . . . not the same thing as making them into smokers.

The third *JAMA* article presented data from a 1990 California telephone survey. The researchers, led by John P. Pierce, head of the University of California at San Diego's Cancer Prevention and Control Program, reported that teenagers were more likely than adults to identify Marlboro or Camel as the most advertised brand. The survey also found that Marlboro's market share increased with age until 24, when it started to decline gradually. Camel, on the other hand, was considerably more popular among teenagers than among young adults. Comparing the California data to the results of a national survey conducted in 1986, Pierce et al. concluded that the market shares for both Marlboro and Camel had increased among adults (the 1986 survey did not include minors). Camel's increase was bigger, particularly among adults under the age of 30 (i.e., the segment R.J. Reynolds claimed to be targeting).

Taken together, these studies suggested that 1) most children know Joe Camel has something to do with cigarettes and 2) the Joe Camel campaign helped increase the brand's market share, especially among young smokers. Since most smokers pick up the habit before they turn 18, it seems likely that the tobacco companies would take an interest in the brand choices of teenagers, and that inference is supported by internal documents. In 1974, for example, Philip Morris hired the Roper Organization to interview young smokers about their brand choices, and more than a third of the 1,879 respondents were described as 18 or younger. "To ensure increased and longer-term growth for Camel filter," said a 1975 RJR memo, "the brand must increase its share penetration among the 14–24 age group, which have a new set of more liberal values and which represent tomorrow's cigarette business." In 1997, as part of an agreement settling state lawsuits, the Liggett Group said tobacco companies have deliberately targeted underage smokers.

The other companies continued to deny that charge. R.J. Reynolds maintained that Joe Camel was aimed at 18-to-24-year-olds, although the company had no way of assuring that he would not also appeal to people younger than 18. In response, David Kessler told ABC's Peter Jennings, "Tell me how you design an advertising campaign that affects only 18-year-olds." Which is sort of the point. If cigarette companies have to avoid any ad that might catch the eye or tickle the fancy of a 16-year-old, they might as well not advertise at all (which would suit Kessler fine). In any case, the important question is whether advertising encourages teenagers to smoke, not whether it steers them toward Camels instead of Marlboros.

In each of the Joe Camel studies, the researchers' conclusions (and the subsequent press coverage) went beyond what the data indicated. Fischer et al., whose comparison between Joe Camel and Mickey Mouse got the most attention, were relatively cautious: "Given the serious health consequences of smoking, the exposure of children to environmental tobacco advertising may represent an important health risk and should be studied further." DiFranza et al. said, "A total ban of tobacco advertising and promotions, as part of an effort to protect children from the dangers of tobacco, can be based on sound scientific reasoning." Pierce et al. flatly concluded that "[c]igarette advertising encourages youth to smoke and should be banned." These are all statements of opinion that have little to do with what the studies actually showed.

Information that came to light in a lawsuit challenging the Joe Camel campaign (a case that R.J. Reynolds settled for $10 million in September 1997) suggests that at least some of the researchers may have prejudged the issue. In a letter he wrote to a coauthor before the research began, DiFranza complained that he had not been able to give reporters "proof that the tobacco companies are advertising to children. I can't point to any one piece of evidence as a smoking gun and say 'here, this proves it.' Well, I have an idea for a project that will give us a couple of smoking guns to bring to the national media." He explained, "I am proposing a quick and easy project that should produce . . . evidence that RJR is going after kids with their Camel ads." Toward the end of the letter, he said, "There, the paper is all ready, now all we need is some data."

Switching arguments

Neither DiFranza's "smoking gun" nor the other studies provided any evidence about the impact of advertising on a teenager's propensity to smoke, which is the crux of the issue. When critics complain that advertising encourages people to smoke, the tobacco companies reply that it encourages smokers to buy particular brands. Strictly speaking, these claims are not mutually exclusive. In principle, advertising can promote an industry's overall sales as well as drum up business for a specific company. An ad for a Compaq portable computer might encourage people to buy a Compaq (the company certainly hopes so), or it might get them thinking about laptops generally. But the tobacco companies argue that the U.S. market for cigarettes is mature, meaning that the product is universally familiar, like toothpaste or deodorant, and attempts to boost overall consumption are no longer cost-effective. Indeed, with smoking rates declining, the tobacco companies are fighting for pieces of a shrinking pie. Tobacco's opponents say this trend makes cigarette manufacturers all the more desperate to maintain their profits; they need advertising like the Joe Camel campaign to attract replacements for smokers who quit or die.

Advocates of an advertising ban contend that brand competition does not adequately explain the industry's spending on advertising and promotion, which totals about $5 billion a year. In 1995, the most recent year for which the Federal Trade Commission has reported figures, coupons, customer premiums (lighters, key chains, clothing, etc.), and allowances to distributors accounted for about 80 percent of this money. Cigarette companies spent about $900 million on newspaper, magazine, outdoor, transit, direct-mail, and point-of-sale advertising.

According to a widely cited article published in the Winter 1987 *Journal of Public Health Policy*, "A simple calculation shows that brand-switching, alone, could never justify the enormous advertising and promotional expenditures of the tobacco companies." Anti-smoking activist Joe B. Tye and his co-authors started with an estimate, based on marketing research, that about 10 percent of smokers switch brands each year. Then they calculated that the industry's spending on advertising and promotion in 1983 amounted to nearly as much per switcher as a typical smoker would have spent on cigarettes that year. They also noted that, since each cigarette maker produces various brands, smokers who switch are not necessarily taking their business to another company.

"Thus," the authors concluded, "advertising and promotion can be considered economically rational only if they perform a defensive function—retaining company brand loyalty that would otherwise be lost to competitors who promote their products—or if they attract new entrants to the smoking marketplace, or discourage smokers from quitting." If defending market share were the only aim, Tye et al. added, the tobacco companies should support a ban on advertising and promotion, which would eliminate the threat from competitors. On the other hand, "If advertising and promotion increase cigarette consumption, then less than two million new or retained smokers—5.5 percent of smokers who start each year or try to quit (most failing)—alone would justify the annual promotional expenditure."

There are several flaws in this argument. To begin with, the estimate for the number of brand switchers does not include people who usually smoke, say, Benson & Hedges but occasionally smoke Camels. Based on its own marketing surveys, R.J. Reynolds reports that about 70 percent of smokers have a second-choice brand that they smoke now and then. About 25 percent regularly buy more than one brand each month. Even smokers who don't have a second favorite sometimes try other brands because of coupons, premiums, and promotional offers.

Another problem is that, in estimating the value of brand switchers, Tye et al. did not take into account the continuing revenue from a new customer; they considered only the money he spends on cigarettes in one year. By contrast, when they estimated the gain from getting someone to start smoking or keeping a smoker who otherwise would have quit, they used the net present value of the additional profit over a 20-year period, which they calculated as $1,085, more than three times a year's revenue.

The one conclusion it seems safe to draw is that many factors other than advertising affect tobacco consumption.

Most important, Tye et al. did not acknowledge that tobacco companies could be competing for new smokers without actually creating them. Although the companies deny that they target minors in any way, building brand loyalty among teenagers is still not the same thing as making them into smokers.

Tye et al. considered the industry's opposition to an advertising ban prima facie evidence that tobacco advertising increases total consumption. But the tobacco companies might also have opposed a ban because it would help delegitimize the industry, opening the way to other kinds of regulation and defeats in product liability suits. Furthermore, a company's attitude toward restrictions on advertising (and brand competition in general) depends on its market position. Philip Morris and R.J. Reynolds, the market leaders, might well be less worried about an advertising ban than their competitors. Tellingly, these were the companies that spearheaded the settlement talks, and they included dramatic restrictions on advertising and promotion in their opening offer.

In any case, it is not clearly foolish for the tobacco companies to spend so much money on advertising and promotion, even without the hope of market expansion. More evidence is necessary to support the claim that tobacco advertising increases consumption. Broadly speaking, there are three ways of investigating this issue. You can look at the historical relationship between changes in advertising and changes in smoking. You can compare smoking trends in places with different levels of advertising. And you can ask people questions in the hope that their answers will suggest how advertising influences attitudes and behavior. None of these approaches has yielded consistent or definitive results. Each has limitations that leave plenty of room for interpretation. The state of the research was aptly, if unintentionally, summed up by the subtitle of a 1994 article in the *International Journal of Advertising* that made the case for a causal link: "The Evidence Is There for Those Who Wish to See It."

Does life imitate ads?

Some analyses of historical data have found a small, statistically significant association between increases in advertising and increases in smoking; others have not. In a 1993 overview of the evidence, Michael Schudson, professor of communication and sociology at the University of California at San Diego, wrote, "In terms of a general relationship between cigarette advertising and cigarette smoking, the available econometric evidence is equivocal and the kind of materials available to produce the evidence leave much to be desired." This sort of research is open to challenge on technical grounds, such as the time period chosen and the methods for measuring advertising and consumption. There is also the possibility that advertising goes up in response to a rise in consumption, rather than the reverse. Industry critics often cite the increases in smoking by women that occurred in the 1920s and the late '60s to early '70s as evidence of advertising's power. "Yet in both cases," Schudson noted, "the advertising campaign followed rather than preceded the behavior it supposedly engendered." In other words, the tobacco companies changed their marketing in response to a trend that was already under way.

International comparisons have also produced mixed results. There is no consistent relationship between restrictions on advertising and smoking rates among adults or minors. In some countries where advertising is severely restricted, such as Sweden, smoking rates are relatively low. In others, such as Norway, they are relatively high. Sometimes smoking drops after advertising is banned; sometimes it doesn't. It is hard to say what such findings mean. Countries where smoking is already declining may be more intolerant of the habit and therefore more likely to ban advertising. Alternatively, a rise in smoking might help build support for a ban. Furthermore, advertising bans are typically accompanied by other measures, such as tobacco tax increases and restrictions on smoking in public, that could be expected to reduce cigarette purchases. The one conclusion it seems safe to draw is that many factors other than advertising affect tobacco consumption.

Surely a nation that proudly allows racist fulminations, communist propaganda, flag burning, nude dancing, pornography, and sacrilegious art can safely tolerate Marlboro caps and Joe Camel T-shirts.

The best way to resolve the issue of advertising's impact on smoking would be a controlled experiment: Take two groups of randomly selected babies; expose one to cigarette advertising but otherwise treat them identically. After 18 years or so, compare smoking rates. Since such a study would be impractical, social scientists have had to make do with less tidy methods, generally involving interviews, questionnaires, or survey data. This kind of research indicates that the most important factors influencing whether a teenager will smoke are the behavior of his peers, his perceptions of the risks and benefits of smoking, and the presence of smokers in his home. Exposure to advertising does not independently predict the decision to smoke, and smokers themselves rarely cite advertising as an important influence on their behavior.

Critics of the industry have been quick to seize upon studies indicating that teenage smokers disproportionately prefer the most advertised cigarette brands. But such research suggests only that advertising has an impact on brand preferences, which the tobacco companies have conceded all along. Several studies have found that teenagers who smoke (or who say they might) are more apt to recall cigarette advertising and to view it favorably. Such findings do not necessarily mean that advertising makes adolescents more likely to smoke. It is just as plausible to suppose that teenagers pay more attention to cigarette ads after they start smoking, or that teenagers who are inclined to smoke for other reasons are also more likely to have a positive view of cigarette ads.

In reporting on research in this area, the mainstream press tends to ignore such alternative interpretations. Consider the coverage of a 1995 study published in the *Journal of the National Cancer Institute*. The study, co-authored by John Pierce, found that teenagers who scored high on a "receptivity" index—which included "recognition of advertising messages, having a favorite advertisement, naming a brand [they] might buy, owning a tobacco-related promotional item, and willingness to use a tobacco-related promotional item"—were more likely to say they could not rule out smoking in the near future. Such "receptivity" was more strongly associated with an inclination to smoke than was smoking among parents and peers.

According to the *New York Times*, these results meant that "[t]obacco advertising is a stronger factor than peer pressure in encouraging children under 18 to smoke." Similarly, the *Boston Globe* reported that the study showed "cigarette advertising has more influence on whether adolescents later start smoking than does having friends or family members who smoke." The Associated Press went even further: "Of all the influences that can draw children into a lifelong habit of smoking, cigarette advertising is the most persuasive." In reality, the study showed only that teenagers who like smoking-related messages and merchandise are more receptive to the idea of smoking—not exactly a startling finding.

A study reported in December 1997 in *Archives of Pediatric and Adolescent Medicine* received similar treatment. The researchers surveyed about 1,200 students in grades six through 12 and found that kids who owned cigarette promotional items such as jackets and backpacks were four times as likely to smoke as those who did not. "Tobacco Gear a Big Draw for Kids," announced the headline in the *Boston Globe*. The story began, "If tobacco manufacturers hope to promote smoking by producing clothing or accessories emblazoned with cigarette logos, research by Dartmouth Medical School suggests that the tactic works well." Under the headline, "Study: Logos Foster Smoking," *Newsday* reported that "children who own cigarette promotional items . . . are far more likely to smoke."

Yet as the researchers themselves conceded, "The finding of an association between CPI [cigarette promotional item] ownership and being a smoker could easily be an expression of an adolescent who acquired these items after having made the decision to become a smoker." Later in the article, they wrote, "Our study and others published to date are subject to the usual limitations inherent in cross-sectional studies, in that we are unable to infer a direction between the exposure (ownership of a CPI) and smoking behavior, limiting our ability to invoke a causal relationship between CPI ownership and smoking." Translation: We would like to say that promotional items make kids smoke, but our study doesn't show that. This shortcoming did not stop the authors from concluding that "all CPI distribution should end immediately."

Unconvincing evidence

Overall, the evidence that advertising plays an important role in getting people to smoke is not very convincing. In 1991 the economist Thomas Schelling, former director of Harvard's Institute for the Study of Smoking Behavior and Policy, said: "I've never seen a genuine study of the subject. Most of the discussion that I hear—even the serious discussion—is about as profound as saying, 'If I were a teenage black girl, that ad would make me smoke.' I just find it altogether unpersuasive. I've been very skeptical that advertising is important in either getting people to smoke or keeping people smoking. It's primarily brand competition." The 1989 surgeon general's report conceded that "[t]here is no scientifically rigorous study available to the public that provides a definitive answer to the basic question of whether advertising and promotion increase the level of tobacco consumption. Given the complexity of the issue, none is likely to be forthcoming in the foreseeable future." The 1994 surgeon general's report, which focused on underage smoking, also acknowledged the "lack of definitive literature."

It's possible, of course, that tobacco advertising has an effect that simply cannot be measured. The 1989 surgeon general's report concluded that, while "the extent of the influence of advertising and promotion on the level of consumption is unknown and possibly unknowable," the weight of the evidence "makes it more likely than not that advertising and promotional activities do stimulate cigarette consumption." The 1994 report, based on suggestive evidence, said "cigarette advertising appears to increase young people's risk of smoking." Similarly, Michael Schudson—who says "[a]dvertising typically attempts little and achieves still less"—argues that cigarette advertising "normally has only slight effect in persuading people to change their attitudes or behaviors." But he adds, "It is reasonable to believe that some teens become smokers or become smokers earlier or become smokers with less guilt or become heavier smokers because of advertising."

Serious critics of tobacco advertising do not subscribe to a simple stimulus-and-response theory in which kids exposed to Joe Camel automatically become smokers. They believe the effects of advertising are subtle and indirect. They argue that the very existence of cigarette ads suggests "it really couldn't be all that bad, or they wouldn't be allowed to advertise," as Elizabeth Whelan of the American Council on Science and Health puts it. They say advertising imagery reinforces the notion, communicated by peers and other role models, that smoking is cool. They say dependence on advertising revenue from tobacco companies discourages magazines from running articles about the health consequences of smoking. They do not claim such effects are sufficient, by themselves, to make people smoke. Rather, they argue that at the margin—say, for an ambivalent teenager whose friends smoke—the influence of advertising may be decisive.

Stated this way, the hypothesis that tobacco advertising increases consumption is impossible to falsify. "Fundamentally," writes Jean J. Boddewyn, a professor of marketing at Baruch College, "one cannot prove that advertising does not cause or influence smoking, because one cannot scientifically prove a negative." So despite the lack of evidence that advertising has a substantial impact on smoking rates, tobacco's opponents can argue that we should play it safe and ban the ads—just in case.

The problem with this line of reasoning is that banning tobacco advertising can be considered erring on the side of caution only if we attach little or no value to freedom of speech. If cigarette ads are a bad influence on kids, that is something for parents and other concerned adults to counter with information and exhortation. They might even consider a serious effort to enforce laws against cigarette sales to minors. But since we clearly are not helpless to resist the persuasive powers of Philip Morris et al.—all of us see the ads, but only some of us smoke—it is hard to square an advertising ban with a presumption against censorship. Surely a nation that proudly allows racist fulminations, communist propaganda, flag burning, nude dancing, pornography, and sacrilegious art can safely tolerate Marlboro caps and Joe Camel T-shirts.

11

The United States Needs a Comprehensive Tobacco Control Policy

William Novelli and Matthew Myers

William Novelli is president and Matthew Myers is vice president and general counsel of the National Center for Tobacco-Free Kids in Washington, D.C.

In June 1998, a congressional bill that would have enacted a comprehensive national tobacco control policy failed in the U.S. Senate. This bill would have required tobacco industry funding of anti-smoking campaigns, restrictions on the advertising and marketing of tobacco products, the granting of authority over tobacco products to the Food and Drug Administration, increased cigarette prices, and promises from the tobacco industry to reduce youth smoking. Moreover, the tobacco industry agreed to pay billions of dollars to states that had sued the industry in the 1990s to recover the health care costs of treating smoking-related illnesses; in turn, cigarette manufacturers would be granted some immunity from future lawsuits. Although opportunities for future legislation still exist, the failure of the McCain bill is a setback for the United States. Civil lawsuits and settlements are unlikely to lead to tobacco control policies that will reduce youth smoking rates and promote public health. The nation is still in need of extensive federal controls on the tobacco industry.

Editor's Note: Although federal tobacco legislation failed in June 1998, the four largest tobacco companies agreed in November 1998 to pay forty-six states $206 billion and submit to advertising and marketing restrictions in the largest civil settlement in history. As of April 1999, a federal lawsuit against the tobacco industry is pending.

In 1998 Congress seriously debated and came very close to passing comprehensive national tobacco control legislation. If we are to be more

Reprinted from William Novelli and Matthew Myers, "The U.S. Tobacco Legislative Imperative," *Multinational Monitor*, October 1998, by permission of *Multinational Monitor*.

successful in the future, we must understand why this opportunity fell short and plan where to go from here.

The legislative debate also exposed divisions in the public health community that prevented us from speaking clearly and doing more to keep the debate focused on saving lives and reining in the outlaw behavior of the tobacco industry. It is vitally important that we understand the choices that divided public health advocates, and take steps to prevent the tobacco industry from using any diversity in views in the future to undermine our ability to act decisively.

The tobacco negotiations

The process that led to the effort to pass comprehensive legislation started in April 1997, when the tobacco industry began serious negotiations with the state attorneys general who had sued the industry in order to recoup Medicaid funds the states had spent treating tobacco-related diseases. The result of the negotiations was a comprehensive agreement in which the tobacco companies agreed to advertising and marketing restrictions; restrictions on youth access to tobacco; tough health warnings; a $500 million per year public education campaign; funding for state and local tobacco control programs; smoking cessation assistance; regulations against environmental tobacco smoke; recognition of the authority of the Food and Drug Administration (FDA) over tobacco products; and stiff penalties if tobacco use among children did not drop by specified levels.

The tobacco industry also agreed to drop court challenges to FDA regulation of tobacco and to the Environmental Protection Agency's risk assessment of second-hand smoke, and to pay $365 billion to be divided between federal public health programs and payments to the states.

In return, the attorneys general agreed to settle their lawsuits as well as pending private class action suits. They further agreed to limitations on future lawsuits, including protection for the tobacco industry from class action suits and punitive damages, and an annual cap on the amount the industry could be forced to pay out in court judgments.

This agreement provoked intense opposition from some tobacco control advocates that focused on the limits the agreement placed on FDA jurisdiction, the adequacy of the payments by the industry and the restrictions placed on litigation against the tobacco companies.

In April 1998, the Senate Commerce Committee passed, by a 19 to 1 margin, a bill sponsored by Senator John McCain that was appreciably stronger than the original agreement. It gave full authority over tobacco products to the FDA, increased the per pack cost to $1.10 and raised the penalties if youth reduction targets were not met. It also eliminated the specific provisions that made it more difficult for victims to recover damages, including the restrictions on class action suits and on punitive damages. While the bill retained an annual cap on the industry's maximum liability annually from court judgments, the cap was increased from the $5 billion in the June 1997 agreement to $6.5 billion.

Initially, it appeared that the McCain bill would pass the Senate, but it faced opposition from those Senators who objected to the expanded role that it gave to the government and to the per pack price increase. There was also less support from the public health community than might have been expected, largely because of the opposition of some of its members to the annual caps, desire for larger penalties against the industry and for a higher per pack price increase. On June 17, 1998, the bill failed by three votes.

Why did the McCain bill fail?

The primary responsibility for the bill's defeat lies with the tobacco industry and its supporters in Congress. The industry again proved the power of campaign contributions and a massive advertising and public relations effort targeted at defeating the bill. It is unfair to blame the public health community for the bill's failure, but the divisions within its ranks aided the efforts of the bill's opponents. Therefore, we need to better understand the choices that weakened the public health community's voice.

There was little disagreement among public health experts about what policies should be enacted to curb tobacco use, but there were strong differences about what was achievable and about when to compromise. Some felt that the power of tobacco control advocates and the public support for action would only grow over time. Therefore, they felt that there was little urgency for Congress to act quickly. Many also believed that compromise was unnecessary because tough legislation could be enacted over the opposition of the tobacco industry. Still others believed that pursuing change at the state level would be more effective.

We supported the federal legislative effort because we believed that there was a serious need for a national tobacco control policy, and that the unique combination of circumstances that created the pressures that led to this opportunity might not be sustained. While we felt that the McCain bill was not perfect, we believed that it was the strongest most far-reaching legislation to be introduced that could be passed. Given the makeup of Congress and the continuing power of the tobacco industry, along with our concern that it would be difficult to maintain the public's intense interest in tobacco control over the long run, we believed that this was an opportunity that should be seized.

> *We still need a comprehensive tobacco control policy that will protect people nationwide and that will rein in the tobacco industry.*

We also felt that there was a need to act now because tobacco use is rising among children and has not been falling among adults to the extent it had previously. Further, only a few states have enacted strong tobacco control policies and the state battles that lie ahead remain difficult and are likely to produce uneven results. We also were concerned that many of the state attorneys general would seek to settle their cases on terms far weaker than the June 1997 agreement rather than go to trial, and that there was a chance the FDA could lose in court. [In November 1998, the four largest tobacco companies and forty-six states agreed to finalize a modified version of the June 1997 settlement.]

The most divisive issue was the legislation's treatment of the tobacco industry's liability. Part of this debate concerned disagreements about what was likely to be achieved in the courts. Some believed that victory in the courts was almost inevitable, would result in the release of additional damaging industry documents and massive punitive damages, and would weaken the tobacco industry to a point that it could no longer exert undue influence on the political process.

In support of tobacco control legislation

We supported comprehensive tobacco control legislation because we were skeptical about the likelihood and ability of the courts to fashion thoughtful, uniform public health policy whether or not the courts ordered the tobacco companies to pay substantial damages. In addition, given that some of the opposition to the McCain bill came from those who oppose government regulation and higher taxes across the board, the fact that the tobacco companies had been weakened by court judgments would not necessarily lead to the legislative implementation of policies as strong as those in the McCain bill. Furthermore, if litigation forced one or more tobacco companies out of business, a new company would step in to fill the market vacuum. Finally, we also believed that victory in court could not be taken for granted. We were concerned that the impact of significant judicial losses might lessen the pressure, which had forced the tobacco industry to make important public health concessions.

The divisions over the tobacco industry's liability went beyond disagreements over the power of the courts, and into the goals to be accomplished through legislation and litigation. Everyone agreed that the tobacco industry does not deserve protection from liability, but as public health advocates, we believed that we should measure each legislative proposal against specific public health goals and principles of social justice, even proposals that included compromise.

From a public health perspective, litigation is a tool to reduce the addiction and death caused by tobacco. To accomplish these goals, litigation can and should make the tobacco industry pay for its past wrongdoing and compensate its victims. It should also serve as a deterrent to future wrongdoing, as a source of information about past misdeeds, and as a mechanism for making the tobacco industry meet accepted business standards.

Not all legislative compromises concerning the tobacco industry's liability, however, undermine these goals. Nor do they necessarily grant the tobacco industry immunity. Some segments of the public health community opposed all legislation that included any liability compromises concerning the tobacco industry. They held this position independent of the legislation's potential positive impact on public health, even if the legislation did not curtail an individual's ability to sue and fully recover damages and even if the legislation did not curtail the judicial system's ability to serve as a deterrent to future wrongdoing. The tobacco industry cited these positions when it argued that the public health community was more interested in promoting the prohibition of tobacco products and the punishment and destruction of the tobacco industry than in promoting the public health.

In summary, a year that began with the opportunity to enact policies to reduce the death toll from tobacco ends with no concrete results. While there will be continued opportunities for progress at the local, state and federal levels, we still need a comprehensive tobacco control policy that will protect people nationwide and that will rein in the tobacco industry. This must be our public health goal.

12

Compromise Between the Government and the Tobacco Industry Would Benefit Public Health

Steven F. Goldstone

Steven F. Goldstone is the chairman and chief executive officer of R.J. Reynolds Nabisco, Incorporated.

In the 1990s, dozens of states filed lawsuits against cigarette manufacturers in an effort to recoup the health care costs of treating smoking-related illnesses. In June 1997, the tobacco industry proposed a global settlement in which they agreed to accept regulation by the Food and Drug Administration, submit to marketing restrictions, fund youth antismoking programs, and pay compensatory damages to states. The tobacco industry is willing to sacrifice capital and marketing freedoms if doing so will resolve the state lawsuits, promote public health, and ensure a measure of future stability for cigarette manufacturers. In the end, tobacco companies should be able to work with public health officials while retaining the right to sell their product to adults.

Editor's Note: This viewpoint was originally presented as a statement before a congressional committee during the January 1998 hearings on the global tobacco settlement that had been proposed in June 1997. Congressional tobacco control legislation failed in June 1998. However, in November 1998, forty-six states and four tobacco companies agreed on a civil settlement based on the June 1997 agreement.

My name is Steven Goldstone. I am the Chairman and Chief Executive Officer of RJR Nabisco, Inc., which owns the Reynolds tobacco company and the Nabisco food company.

I came to RJR Nabisco a little over two years ago [in 1995] after leav-

Reprinted from Steven F. Goldstone, testimony before the U.S. House Committee on Commerce, 105th Cong., 2nd sess., January 29, 1998.

ing the New York law firm where I had practiced law for twenty-five years.

While my legal practice was unrelated to tobacco issues, I nevertheless came to RJR with the firm belief that tobacco companies can and should be able to offer their products to adult customers—so long as they are sensitive to public health concerns, and are prepared to accept the responsibilities of working with government and public health officials. That's true even when, on the surface, it would seem to be in conflict with what's in the tobacco company's narrow financial interest.

My view is simple. When you sell a legal product with significant health risks, you should be cooperating with government—not fighting it.

Balancing business and public health policy

In my early months as chief executive, I thought long and hard about how to balance this belief with my responsibilities to thousands of shareholders, as well as my obligations to 80,000 employees and thousands of retirees. I also had to consider the important interests of other people affected by this business: growers, distributors, retailers and customers.

This is a business unlike any other business. The tobacco company sells a legal product that presents known health risks to smokers. At the same time, the country needs a sound, advanced public health policy that educates people about all the issues concerning tobacco products. I believe the two are not incompatible.

I would like to explain how my attempt to balance them has led to RJR Nabisco's participation in the proposal you are considering today. But before I do so, I want to talk to you about the documents from Reynolds that have been commented upon so much in the last two weeks [of January 1998]. They have been a source of great concern to me as the new CEO of RJR Nabisco, just as they should also be to the members of this Committee and the American public. [In January 1998, RJR released old documents detailing the company's intent to market cigarettes to minors.]

Tobacco companies can and should be able to offer their products to adult customers—so long as they are sensitive to public health concerns.

I am not going to attempt to defend each of those documents. It is simply not acceptable under any circumstance to review, much less commission, marketing research on minors. It has never been acceptable, or in my view ethical, to target underage smokers. Reynolds' management understands this and understands that there is no place in our company for anyone who cannot accept and live by these fundamental principles. I am confident that all people at Reynolds—who are honest, dedicated people with responsible values—know the proper boundaries and make the right decisions when it comes to the marketing of tobacco products.

It would be fair to evaluate these documents in the context of the time in which they were created—and in the environment in which they were created. Many of these documents are more than twenty years old. In the 1970's, our country had different attitudes about smoking from those we have today. In forty percent of the states, there were no restrictions on the sale of tobacco products to minors or the minimum age was lower than eighteen. In fact, many public high schools had designated smoking areas. Today that is inconceivable and certainly unacceptable from a public health point of view, and also to a majority of the American people.

As Congress considers the Proposed Resolution, I am sure it will continue to debate the meaning of these documents and there will be disagreement as to the proper conclusions to be drawn from them, since they represent only a few of the millions of pages of documents in the litigation record. The litigation over these old documents points out to me, however, the importance of resolving past disagreements—if we can— and deciding to move forward together to solve the problems tobacco's critics see in this material.

That's why I'd like to come back to tell you how RJR came to participate in the process leading to the Proposed Resolution which is before you today.

I was not long on my new job before I came to the belief that all of us would have been better served in any number of instances if there had been a more civil discussion of the hard issues posed by tobacco products. But there wasn't. We have for years had instead an adversarial environment, marked by distrust and controversy. The result is that today we wrestle with a series of tough, fundamental decisions for you to make on behalf of the American people, fifty million of whom use tobacco products, and for me to make on behalf of thousands of employees and shareholders.

When I first arrived at RJR Nabisco, I was astounded at the intensity of the emotion, the constant attacks, the charges and counter-charges, the harsh rhetoric—a general lack of civility and endless litigation. From my perspective, this was not a fight our company should be in because in the end, I could not see how anyone really would win. The tobacco industry had been winning lawsuits for forty years and victories certainly did not create a reasonable business environment.

On the other hand, I also thought about the people who in good faith are trying to define and advance legitimate public health concerns. Again, there was no constructive dialogue. Litigation and press releases were the main tools in use. I questioned whether, from the government and public health perspective, they could possibly be satisfied with the prospect of another forty years of the same conflicts with no real resolution.

So we asked, what could the world look like if we put on the table our traditional rights and freedoms as a company in a free enterprise system— many of which are protected by the Constitution—in order to address dramatically the well-founded national concern about children's smoking? What if we were willing to give up marketing freedoms—especially critical to Reynolds, trying as it is to reverse a long-term decline in competitive position?

Putting freedoms on the negotiating table

It is difficult for me to underestimate the competitive challenges our domestic tobacco business faced. Its market share was not only declining but so were its earnings. In 1992, its operating earnings were $2.2 billion. By

1996, they had sunk to $1.4 billion. Nevertheless, for the first time in over twenty years, Reynolds was starting to strengthen its position. As in any consumer product company, to maintain that momentum Reynolds needed strong advertising and marketing tools to communicate to adult customers.

Yet, we ultimately did put these freedoms on the negotiating table in an effort to get to a comprehensive resolution of the tobacco controversy.

Even further, what would the world look like if we agreed to pay enormous and unprecedented amounts of money, forever, to end finally the years of litigation? There is no question there would be severe price increases, steep declines in volume and serious negative impact on Reynolds' earnings.

Yet, we ultimately ended up putting these enormous sums of money on the negotiating table.

Our tobacco company is willing to agree to the very substantial restrictions on marketing, even to adults, the new FDA regulatory and enforcement authority over tobacco products, and the payment of the huge amounts of money required by the Proposed Resolution, if we can resolve some of the massive litigation and bring a measure of predictability and stability to the future. But it's risky for us in the extreme.

I am not certain how successful Reynolds can be in stemming dramatic earnings declines in the new business environment that this agreement will usher in. But I believe—and the people at my company agree—that a future that is more predictable and less controversial should be in our best interest. That means at RJR Nabisco we will be able to allocate capital over time to businesses with the potential to provide an acceptable return for shareholders, as our domestic tobacco business is expected to decline. It means we will have the flexibility to consider restructuring steps with the knowledge that litigation risks are manageable. It will undoubtedly mean that the domestic tobacco business will become less significant to us strategically.

> *Our tobacco company is willing to agree to . . . substantial restrictions on marketing . . . if we can resolve some of the massive litigation and bring a measure of predictability and stability to the future.*

At the same time, I cannot, speaking for my company, prudently agree to even more crushing economic burdens on the tobacco company's business. We want to be part of a new day of balanced and practical regulation, but I cannot, consistent with my own duties and responsibilities that I talked about earlier, agree on a course of action that would clearly and inevitably destroy the viability of this company.

When the Chairman of Philip Morris and I met [in April 1997] with the state attorneys general and other interested parties, it was in an effort to break down barriers, to share points of view, and to determine whether we could sketch out a framework for this new direction. That led to many months of often tough discussions, resulting in a complicated but comprehensive agreement—one that was far more onerous and expensive than I anticipated, but that is what can happen in a tough negotiation.

The issue now is in the hands of Congress. You have the final and most important voice whether to implement the settlement reached by the state attorneys general, representatives of the public health community, the trial lawyers and the tobacco industry.

I hope my explanation helps you to reach a decision that will lead to:

- A dramatic reduction in the use of tobacco products by minors;
- Clear and extensive regulation by the Food and Drug Administration over the manufacture, marketing and sale of tobacco products;
- Settlement of massive tort litigation; and
- Reaffirmation of the rights of adults to make informed choices to use tobacco products as they desire.

Since the negotiations began, I have given these issues a lot of thought. I do not know of another way to resolve them.

We are committed to supporting the Proposed Resolution and abiding fully by its terms.

It is time to end the fighting and move in a new direction. We stand at an important crossroad. One path keeps us on the forty year road of conflict and confrontation which benefits no one. The other path provides for extraordinary gains in public health policy and fundamental change for the industry. This is a unique opportunity for all of us to be part of the solution.

13

The Tobacco Settlement Is Commendable

Hubert H. Humphrey III

Hubert H. Humphrey III is the attorney general of Minnesota.

On November 23, 1998, the tobacco industry agreed to pay forty-six states $206 billion and submit to advertising and marketing restrictions in a large civil settlement—the result of lawsuits on the part of states attempting to recover the costs of treating smoking-related illnesses. Although this agreement is not a perfect way to address the problems caused by tobacco use, it is somewhat of a victory for the states because they will receive partial compensation for the health care costs of smoking. However, more actions must be taken to reduce youth smoking, including granting the Food and Drug Administration regulatory control over nicotine, increasing cigarette taxes, and developing effective antismoking public health programs.

The tobacco agreement signed on November 23, 1998, by the nation's attorneys general does not drive a stake through the heart of the big tobacco companies. It does not even change the status quo dramatically. Still, it is a victory for the states and their attorneys general.

A victory for the states

The states win because the settlement will compensate them, at least in part, for the costs of providing medical treatment to residents harmed by tobacco. The attorneys general come out ahead, too. Until now, if they tried difficult cases and won, they had to pay huge fees to the plaintiff's outside lawyers. If they lost, they looked like failures for having passed up billions in settlement dollars. From now on, they will be spared having to decide whether to try more cases.

On the other hand, the new agreement will prevent states from achieving full justice against tobacco manufacturers. The tobacco companies are winners because they no longer will face the most immediate threat of catastrophic judgments. The lump sum the industry has agreed to pay can easily be met by raising the price of cigarettes so gradually that demand will not fall off.

And since potential competitors will be required to assume some of the burden of the settlement, the big tobacco companies need not fear the advent of new companies that might cut into their market shares by producing less harmful tobacco.

Still far to go

What is good news for the tobacco industry has never been good news for public health. The settlement imposes only minor new restrictions on the industry's continuing effort to hook new nicotine users. The use of cartoon figures in advertising is now prohibited. But judging from the experience of those countries where all advertising is banned but teen-agers still light up in droves, limits on advertising may not make much difference.

The settlement, in sum, demonstrates how far we have to go. If we are to reduce smoking among the young, several changes must take place.

The medical community has now reached a consensus that nicotine use should be severely reduced or even eliminated. Most people who use tobacco wish they could quit. The industry knows this and will fight to keep their customers addicted. Thus, Congress must grant regulatory authority over nicotine to the Food and Drug Administration.

Tobacco companies pay lip service to reducing under-age use but have never policed retailers to make sure they keep cigarettes out of the hands of under-age smokers. Congress must pass a meaningful "youth look-back" provision that would keep track of tobacco use by minors and penalize the industry if use does not decline.

Congress and the states must also increase taxes on tobacco products. This is a bitter pill for many adult smokers. But study after study has shown that sharp price increases suppress demand, especially among minors.

Although the tobacco industry has not been struck a crippling blow, the states have made advances that would have seemed unattainable a few years ago.

State legislatures also have a part to play. They must reinvest their tobacco dollars in developing and administering effective tobacco-control programs. In Minnesota, polls show overwhelming public support for spending most or even all of the money won in the settlement on public health programs. If the $206 billion the states are scheduled to receive over the next 25 years is wisely invested by legislatures in public health, particularly in anti-tobacco efforts, future generations may be saved from becoming addicted to this deadly drug.

Although the tobacco industry has not been struck a crippling blow, the states have made advances that would have seemed unattainable a few years ago. It is now up to Congress to show the same aggressiveness and creativity that the attorneys general have showed in tackling on the greatest public health problem of our time.

14

The Tobacco Settlement Is Not Commendable

Robert J. Samuelson

Robert J. Samuelson is a nationally syndicated columnist.

The 1998 tobacco settlement, in which tobacco companies have agreed to pay partial compensation to states for the health care costs of treating smoking-related illnesses, is counterproductive. For one thing, the resulting increase in cigarette prices will unfairly tax smokers, many of whom are poor. Furthermore, the agreement will further confuse the public about who should bear the ultimate responsibility for the consequences of smoking: the individual, the government, or the tobacco industry. Unfortunately, moreover, the success of the antismoking campaign of the 1990s is likely to encourage misguided attacks on the manufacturers of other legal but risky products such as alcohol and high-fat food.

We may have closure—at least temporarily—to the anti-smoking crusade of the 1990s. The agreement between state attorneys general and the tobacco companies for the industry to pay the states roughly $200 billion over 25 years may quiet the controversy.

If so, this will be the agreement's main benefit, because otherwise it is a parody of good government policy. It imposes a steep tax on a heavily poor part of the population; it offers only modest health benefits; and it deepens popular confusion about the public consequences of smoking.

Let's concede the small possible health gains. The agreement will raise cigarette prices; tobacco analyst Martin Feldman of Salomon Smith Barney figures that retail prices will go from an average $2.07 a pack in 1998 to $2.90 in the year 2000. Higher prices might reduce the number of smokers by a few percentage points of the population.

Let's also note that the agreement aids the tobacco industry. By reducing the threat of lawsuits, it bolsters companies' stock prices. Still, the great myth of this struggle is that, just because cigarettes are unhealthy and the tobacco industry is often dishonest, the people on the other side must be morally superior.

In truth, they—meaning plaintiffs' lawyers, politicians and public-health advocates—also frequently pursue their goals with a single-minded dishonesty and hypocrisy. And their motives are often selfish: personal enrichment (the lawyers); power and popularity (the politicians and public-health advocates).

Little wonder the results are disheartening. Almost everyone has long known that smoking is dangerous. In 1954, 70 percent of the public thought smoking "harmful" and 42 percent thought it "one of the causes of lung cancer"; by 1990, these responses were 96 percent and 94 percent. Most Americans also think that smokers decide for themselves whether to smoke. A 1997 poll asked who is "more responsible for . . . smoking-related illnesses," smokers or tobacco companies. By 76 percent to 17 percent, respondents said smokers.

Is society entitled to penalize smokers?

The debate's central issue ought to be: How much is society entitled to penalize smokers for their decisions, because those decisions are deemed unhealthy? Should present smokers be punished (via higher taxes) to deter future smokers? These hard questions pit Americans' belief in personal freedom against the desire to protect public health.

Precisely because the questions are hard, anti-smoking advocates diverted the debate to three other ideas, all dubious.

First, smokers aren't responsible for their behavior because smoking is addictive.

Second, smoking creates huge social costs—mainly higher health spending—that nonsmokers pay through higher taxes.

Finally, the tobacco industry should be punished and forced to compensate nonsmokers for smoking's social costs.

Well. Even if smoking is addictive, people can—often with much pain and hard work—break addictions. There are now more ex-smokers than smokers.

As for higher government costs, studies have shown that—because smokers die earlier than nonsmokers—they create savings for government through lower lifetime health and pension costs.

Public-health advocates covet extra money for pet [antismoking] programs; and lawyers crave their fees. All this has involved an adept manipulation of courts and legislatures.

But suppose smokers lack free will and raise government's costs. Still, the industry could not pay those costs directly without going bankrupt. The money always has had to come from smokers through higher cigarette prices—the equivalent of a tax increase.

Anti-smoking advocates rarely discuss this, because the implications are devastating.

Smokers have low incomes. Only 20 percent of cigarette taxes are paid by those with incomes over $50,000; 34 percent are paid by those

with incomes under $20,000 and 19 percent by those with incomes be-
tween $20,000 and $30,000.

Moreover, smokers already pay steep federal and state cigarette taxes
(now averaging about 58 cents a pack) that more than cover any possible
public costs they create.

As a result, the anti-smoking crusade becomes a reverse Robin Hood
arrangement: It sanctifies soak-the-poor taxes and robs the poor to pay
the rich. The attorneys general's agreement now enshrines this.

The rich, of course, are the private lawyers who represent the states in
their tobacco suits.

The agreement allows up to $500 million in annual fees for perhaps
a few hundred and at most a few thousand lawyers. For how long? Arbi-
trators will decide.

The cigarette dispute has evolved into a welfare program that may
create some instant billionaires and many multimillionaires.

Because none of this can be defended, it is camouflaged. For self-
interested reasons, the anti-smoking advocates never openly described
public choices. Beyond taxing smokers to cut smoking, politicians want
to keep the taxes—and not to rebate them.

Public-health advocates covet extra money for pet programs; and
lawyers crave their fees. All this has involved an adept manipulation of
courts and legislatures.

A gullible public—aided by a pliant press—embraced the anti-smoking
hysteria. Because the campaign succeeded, it will inspire assaults against
other industries. We can't tell the target (whether alcohol, or autos or fatty
foods) or the tactics. But it's just a matter of time.

Organizations to Contact

The editors have compiled the following list of organizations concerned with the issues debated in this book. The descriptions are derived from materials provided by the organizations. All have publications or information available for interested readers. The list was compiled on the date of publication of the present volume; the information provided here may change. Be aware that many organizations take several weeks or longer to respond to inquiries, so allow as much time as possible.

Action on Smoking and Health (ASH)
2013 H St. NW, Washington, DC 20006
(202) 659-4310
website: http://www.ash.org

Action on Smoking and Health promotes the rights of nonsmokers and works to protect them from the harms of smoking. ASH worked to eliminate tobacco ads from radio and television and to ban smoking in airplanes, buses, and many public places. The organization publishes the bimonthly newsletter *ASH Smoking and Health Review* and fact sheets on a variety of topics, including teen smoking, passive smoking, and nicotine addiction.

American Cancer Society
1599 Clifton Rd. NE, Atlanta, GA 30329
(800) ACS-2345 (227-2345)
website: http://www.cancer.org

The American Cancer Society is one of the primary organizations in the United States devoted to educating the public about cancer and to funding cancer research. The society spends a great deal of its resources on educating the public about the dangers of smoking and on lobbying for antismoking legislation. The American Cancer Society makes available hundreds of publications, ranging from reports and surveys to position papers.

American Council on Science and Health (ACSH)
1995 Broadway, 2nd Fl., New York, NY 10023-5860
(212) 362-7044 • fax: (212) 362-4919
e-mail: acsh@acsh.org • website: http://www.acsh.org

ACSH is a consumer education group concerned with issues related to food, nutrition, chemicals, pharmaceuticals, lifestyle, the environment, and health. It publishes the quarterly newsletter *Priorities* as well as the booklets *The Tobacco Industry's Use of Nicotine as a Drug* and *Marketing Cigarettes to Kids*.

Americans for Nonsmokers' Rights
2530 San Pablo Ave., Suite J, Berkeley, CA 94702
(510) 841-3032 • fax: (510) 841-3071
e-mail: anr@no-smoke.org • website: http://www.no-smoke.org

Americans for Nonsmokers' Rights seeks to protect the rights of nonsmokers in the workplace and other public settings. It works with the American Nonsmokers' Rights Foundation, which promotes smoking prevention, non-smokers' rights, and public education about secondhand smoke. The organization publishes the quarterly newsletter *ANR Update*, the book *Clearing the Air*, and the guidebook *How to Butt In: Teens Take Action.*

American Smokers Alliance (ASA)
PO Box 189, Bellvue, CO 80512
fax: (970) 493-4253
e-mail: derf@smokers.org • website: http://www.smokers.org

The American Smokers Alliance is a nonprofit organization of volunteers who believe that nonsmokers and smokers have equal rights. ASA strives to unify existing smokers' rights efforts, combat antitobacco legislation, fight discrimination against smokers in the workplace, and encourage individuals to become involved in local smokers' rights movements. It publishes articles and news bulletins, including *Smokers Have Reduced Risks of Alzheimer's and Parkinson's Disease* and *Lung Cancer Can Be Eliminated!*

Canadian Council for Tobacco Control (CCTC)
170 Laurier Ave. W, Suite 1000, Ottawa, ON K1P 5V5 CANADA
(800) 267-5234 • (613) 567-3050 • fax: (613) 567-5695
e-mail: info-services@cctc.ca • website: http://www.cctc.ca/ncth

The CCTC works to ensure a healthier society, free from addiction and involuntary exposure to tobacco products. It promotes a comprehensive tobacco control program involving educational, social, fiscal, and legislative interventions. It publishes several fact sheets, including *Promoting a Lethal Product* and *The Ban on Smoking on School Property: Successes and Challenges.*

Competitive Enterprise Institute (CEI)
1001 Connecticut Ave. NW, Suite 1250, Washington, DC 20036
(202) 331-1010 • fax: (202) 331-0640
e-mail: info@cei.org • website: http://www.cei.org

The institute is a pro–free market public interest group involved in a wide range of issues, including tobacco. CEI questions the validity and accuracy of Environmental Protection Agency studies that report the dangers of secondhand smoke. Its publications include books, monographs, policy studies, and the monthly newsletter *CEI Update.*

drkoop.com
8920 Business Park Dr., Suite 200, Austin, TX 78759
(888) 795-0998 • (512) 726-5110 • fax: (512) 726-5130
e-mail: feedback@drkoop.com • website: http://www.drkoop.com/tobacco

Based on the vision of former U.S. Surgeon General Dr. C. Everett Koop, drkoop.com is a consumer-focused interactive website that provides users with comprehensive healthcare information on a wide variety of subjects, including tobacco. The organization publishes reports, fact sheets, press releases, and books, including *The No-Nag, No-Guilt, Do-It-Your-Own-Way Guide to Quitting Smoking.*

Environmental Protection Agency (EPA)
Indoor Air Quality Information Clearinghouse
PO Box 37133, Washington, DC 20013-7133
(800) 438-4318 • (202) 484-1307 • fax: (202) 484-1510
e-mail: iaqinfo@aol.com • website: http://www.epa.gov/iaq

The EPA is the agency of the U.S. government that coordinates actions designed to protect the environment. It promotes indoor air quality standards that reduce the dangers of secondhand smoke. The EPA publishes and distributes reports such as *Respiratory Health Effects of Passive Smoking: Lung Cancer and Other Disorders* and *What You Can Do About Secondhand Smoke as Parents, Decisionmakers, and Building Occupants.*

Fight Ordinances & Restrictions to Control & Eliminate Smoking (FORCES)
PO Box 591257, San Francisco, CA 94159
(415) 824-4716
e-mail: info@forces.org • website: http://www.forces.org

FORCES fights against smoking ordinances and restrictions designed to eventually eliminate smoking, and it works to increase public awareness of smoking-related legislation. It opposes any state or local ordinance it feels is not fair to those who choose to smoke. Although FORCES does not advocate smoking, it asserts that an individual has the right to choose to smoke and that smokers should be accommodated where and when possible. FORCES publishes *Tobacco Weekly* as well as many articles.

Group Against Smoking Pollution (GASP)
PO Box 632, College Park, MD 20741-0632
(301) 459-4791

Consisting of nonsmokers adversely affected by tobacco smoke, GASP works to promote the rights of nonsmokers, to educate the public about the problems of secondhand smoke, and to encourage the regulation of smoking in public places. The organization provides information and referral services and distributes educational materials, buttons, posters, and bumper stickers. GASP publishes booklets and pamphlets such as *The Nonsmokers' Bill of Rights* and *The Nonsmokers' Liberation Guide.*

National Center for Tobacco-Free Kids/Campaign for Tobacco-Free Kids
1707 L St. NW, Suite 800, Washington, DC 20036
(800) 284-KIDS (284-5437)
e-mail: info@tobaccofreekids.org • website: http://www.tobaccofreekids.org

The National Center for Tobacco-Free Kids/Campaign for Tobacco-Free Kids is the largest private initiative ever launched to protect children from tobacco addiction. The center works in partnership with the American Cancer Society, American Heart Association, American Medical Association, the National PTA, and over 100 other health, civic, corporate, youth, and religious organizations. Among the center's publications are press releases, reports, and fact sheets, including *Tobacco Use Among Youth, Tobacco Marketing to Kids,* and *Smokeless (Spit) Tobacco and Kids.*

U.S. Food and Drug Administration (FDA)
Rockville, MD 20857
(800) 532-4440 • (301) 443-1130 • fax: (301) 443-9767
e-mail: execsec@oc.fda.gov • website: http://www.fda.gov

As the agency of the U.S. government charged with protecting the health of the public against impure and unsafe foods, drugs, cosmetics, and other potential hazards, the FDA has sought the regulation of nicotine as a drug and has investigated manipulation of nicotine levels in cigarettes by the tobacco industry. It provides copies of congressional testimony given in the debate over the regulation of nicotine.

Bibliography

Books

William Everett Bailey   *The Invisible Drug.* Cincinnati, OH: Mosaic, 1996.

California Environmental Protection Agency   *Health Effects of Exposure to Environmental Tobacco Smoke: Final Report.* Sacramento, CA: The Office, 1997.

John Fahs   *Cigarette Confidential: The Unfiltered Truth about the Ultimate American Addiction.* New York: Berkeley, 1996.

A. Lee Fritschler   *Smoking and Politics: Policy Making and the Federal Bureaucracy.* Upper Saddle River, NJ: Prentice Hall, 1996.

David G. Gilbert   *Smoking: Individual Differences, Psychopathology, and Emotion.* Washington, DC: Taylor and Francis, 1995.

Stanton A. Glantz   *The Cigarette Papers.* Berkeley and Los Angeles: University of California Press, 1996.

Mark S. Gold   *Tobacco.* New York: Plenum Medical, 1995.

Emma Haughton   *A Right to Smoke?* New York: Watts, 1997.

Philip J. Hilts   *Smokescreen: The Truth Behind the Tobacco Industry Cover-Up.* Reading, MA: Addison-Wesley, 1996.

Peter D. Jacobson and Jeffrey Wasserman   *Tobacco Control Laws: Implementation and Enforcement.* Santa Monica, CA: RAND, 1997.

Richard Kluger   *Ashes to Ashes: America's Hundred-Year Cigarette War, the Public Health, and the Unabashed Triumph of Philip Morris.* New York: Knopf, 1996.

Susan S. Lang and Beth H. Marks   *Teens and Tobacco: A Fatal Attraction.* New York: Twenty-First Century Books, 1996.

Carrick Mollenkamp et al.   *The People vs. Big Tobacco: How the States Took On the Cigarette Giants.* Princeton, NJ: Bloomberg, 1998.

Jacob Sullum   *For Your Own Good: The Anti-Smoking Crusade and the Tyranny of Public Health.* New York: Free Press, 1998.

W. Kip Viscusi   *Smoking: Making the Risky Decision.* New York: Oxford University Press, 1993.

Elizabeth M. Whelan, ed.   *Cigarettes: What the Warning Label Doesn't Tell You: The First Comprehensive Guide to the Health Consequences of Smoking.* Amherst, NY: Prometheus Books, 1997.

World Health Organization   *Tobacco or Health: A Global Status Report.* Geneva: World Health Organization, 1997.

Periodicals

Joseph L. Andrews	"How to Kick a National Habit," *Humanist*, May 15, 1997.
Carl E. Bartecchi, Thomas D. Mackenzie, and Robert W. Schrier	"The Human Costs of Tobacco Use," Part I, *New England Journal of Medicine*, March 31, 1994. Available from 10 Shattuck St., Boston, MA 02115-6094.
Sally Beatty	"Tobacco Industry Agrees to Ad Loopholes," *Wall Street Journal*, November 17, 1998.
Ernest Beck	"Ad Bans Abroad Haven't Snuffed Out Smoking," *Wall Street Journal*, June 12, 1997.
John E. Calfee	"Why the War on Tobacco Will Fail," *Weekly Standard*, July 20, 1998. Available from News America Publishing, Inc., 1211 Avenue of the Americas, New York, NY 10036.
David W. Cowles	"The Price of Smoking," *Newsweek*, February 1, 1999.
Barbara Dority	"The Rights of Joe Camel and the Marlboro Man," *Humanist*, January/February 1997.
John R. Garrison	"Yes: Scientific Research Shows Overwhelmingly That Other People's Smoke Can Hurt You," *Insight*, June 16, 1997. Available from 3600 New York Ave. NE, Washington, DC 20002.
Stanton A. Glantz	"The Anti-Smoking Campaign That Tobacco Loves," *Harper's*, July 1996.
Steven F. Goldstone	"The Failure of the Tobacco Legislation," *Vital Speeches of the Day*, October 1, 1998.
Stephen Goode	"Call It a 'Stinking Weed,' Just Don't Try to Ban It," *Insight*, June 16, 1997.
Issues and Controversies on File	"Tobacco Settlement," November 20, 1998. Available from Facts On File News Services, 11 Penn Plaza, New York, NY 10001-2006.
Kathiann Kowalski	"Tobacco's Toll on Teens," *Current Health*, February 1997.
Dwight R. Lee	"The Government's Crusade Against Tobacco: Can It Ultimately Succeed?" *USA Today Magazine*, May 1, 1998.
John J. Lynch and Thomas Humber	"Do We Need a Tobacco Bill?" *World & I*, July 1998. Available from 3600 New York Ave. NE, Washington, DC 20002.
Kai Maristed	"Nicotine, An Autobiography," *American Scholar*, Summer 1996.
John McCain and Robert A. Levy	"Q: Should Congress Decide the Future of the Tobacco Industry?" *Insight*, May 11, 1998.
Barry Meier	"Lost Horizons: The Billboard Prepares to Give Up Smoking," *New York Times*, April 19, 1999.
Lorraine Mooney	"Smoking Out Bad Science," *Wall Street Journal*, March 19, 1998.

Mother Jones	Special report on the politics of tobacco, May/June 1996.
Salim Muwakkil	"Black Lungs," *In These Times*, June 14, 1998.
William D. Novelli	"Tobacco Control: The Dramatic Choice," *Science*, October 10, 1997.
John P. Pierce et al.	"Tobacco Industry Promotion of Cigarettes and Adolescent Smoking," *JAMA*, February 18, 1998. Available from Subscriber Services Center, American Medical Association, 515 N. State St., Chicago, IL 60610.
Andrew Bard Schmookler	"Calculating the Individual's Cost of Smoking," *Christian Science Monitor*, April 22, 1997.
Joseph P. Shapiro	"Industry Foes Fume over Tobacco Deal," *U.S. News & World Report*, November 30, 1998.
Randolph D. Smoak Jr.	"The AMA's Tobacco Fight," *Vital Speeches of the Day*, February 1, 1996.
Jacob Sullum	"Just How Bad Is Secondhand Smoke?" *National Review*, May 16, 1994.
Jacob Sullum	"What the Doctor Orders," *Reason*, January 1996.
David Tannenbaum and Robert Weissman	Special issue on the Tobacco Papers, *Multinational Monitor*, July/August 1998.
Saundra Torry	"Philip Morris's Smoke Signals to Teens," *Washington Post National Weekly Edition*, April 5, 1999. Available from 1150 15th St. NW, Washington, DC 20071.
Elizabeth M. Whelan	"Is a Deal with the Cigarette Industry in the Interest of Public Health?" *Priorities*, vol. 9, no. 2, 1997. Available from the American Council on Science and Health, 1995 Broadway, 2nd Fl., New York, NY 10023-5860.

Index